The complete life story of the first
Aerospace Nurse, a pioneer in the world's
most exciting profession for women!

Dee O'Hara
ASTRONAUTS'
NURSE

by Virginia B. McDonnell, R.N.

A RUTLEDGE BOOK

THOMAS NELSON & SONS
Edinburgh • New York • Toronto

All pictures except those listed as follows are by courtesy of
The National Aeronautics and Space Administration (NASA)
Radioplane a Division of Northrop Corp. Page 16
Providence Hospital Page 33 — The New York Daily News Page 46
United Press International Page 96
Wide World Page 114 — U.S. Air Force Page 119
A. Devaney, Inc. Pages 38 and 62
Pete Corvallis, The Portland Oregonian Pages 24, 50 and 104

CONTENTS

For Alan Shepard, the long wait—countdown for the first launching

Chapter 1

COUNTDOWN

Date: 5 May, 1961. Time: 0614 (6:14 A.M.) Eastern Daylight Time. Place: Cape Canaveral (now Cape Kennedy), Florida. Mission: To launch the first American astronaut into space . . . and to recover safely both man and aircraft.

All around the world, television sets showed the 37-year-old Navy commander, Alan B. Shepard Jr., as he stepped from a van and moved briskly to the elevator that would carry him up through the gantry, up 65 feet to his capsule, *Freedom 7*. In his silvery pressure suit and helmet, he might have been the hero of a science-fiction novel.

"It's go for broke," murmured 2nd Lieutenant Dee O'Hara, America's only areospace nurse, on loan from the U.S. Air Force Nurse Corps to the National Aeronautics and Space Administration (NASA).

Like thousands of engineers, scientists, researchers, technicians, public-information officers and, of course, doctors engaged in Project Mercury, Dee O'Hara had her own unique and vital role in the mission. Like those other thousands, she felt a choking tension as the minutes of countdown ticked by.

Lieutenant Dee O'Hara was at her post in the Forward Medical Station—the blockhouse. It was a reinforced concrete structure, designed to provide protection against blast, heat or an explosion.

Also in the blockhouse that May morning were a surgeon, an anesthesiologist, two corpsmen, and another Air Force nurse, 1st Lieutenant Shirley Sineath, Dee's roommate. Shirley's special responsibility for Project Mercury was to prepare instruments and equipment for down-range hospitals and recovery ships.

This particular team-within-a-team was standing by to monitor the astronaut's physical condition by means of various dials and graphs, and to give him aid in the event of a disaster . . . if there were anything left of him. In case of an explosion, there would be many, many other patients—but they would be cared for by the Pan American World Airways medical-nursing team, which assumed responsibility for all personnel other than the astronaut himself.

"I won't think of the possibility of a catastrophe," Dee thought. But how could she help herself?

Commander Shepard and his backup pilot, Colonel John H. Glenn Jr., were in their quarters on the second floor of Hangar S, about 3 miles from the launch pad. They continued their low residue diets. They underwent their final physical examinations. If Al Shepard developed a last-minute ailment, John Glenn would be ready to take his place with no delay to the launch.

On launch day minus one—yesterday—the two astronauts had gone over the check list of procedures.

Dee O'Hara was with them during most of their waking hours before countdown. As a nurse, she kept a close eye out for any signs of physical disability. And part of her job was to keep outsiders away from her charges. Outsiders might easily bring in germs. At the very least, they could cause increased tension.

Hundreds of press representatives swarmed over the area. A frequently asked question was whether the prolonged pre-flight period had any effect on the astronaut's frame of mind.

A public-information officer from NASA answered that one by saying that the project officials were "not too worried about either the commander or his alternate." The pilots were accustomed to long waiting periods before launch. However, he added realistically, there was very definite concern that the presence of hundreds of newsmen might cause tension.

He drove home the point by relating an episode that had occurred some months back. A technician had

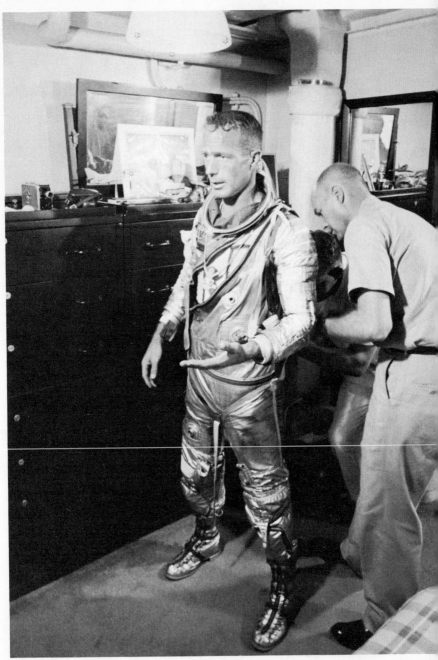

Over at last! Mercury pilot Scott Carpenter is helped out of his space suit after the spectacular first space flight

been ready to throw a certain switch during a simulated launching countdown. At the crucial moment, he spotted a battery of cameras trained on him. Momentarily distracted, he threw the switch the wrong way.

"This could be fatal," the officer warned bluntly.

Dee O'Hara had made up her mind that no one was going to get near her astronauts at this most important of all moments. She locked the door. NASA managers agreed with her and the door remained locked.

"The fellows" had their privacy. They slept. The countdown began at 3 A.M. on 5 May. Together, Shepard and Glenn breakfasted on eggs, filet mignon wrapped in bacon, orange juice, coffee and toast.

It was time to go to the suiting room. Each man had long since been tattooed at four places on his body. The tattoo marks would facilitate the placing of the electrocardiogram sensors. The sensors, in turn, would connect with monitoring equipment.

The Mercury program was going to provide the free world with its first opportunity for full-time monitoring of a man in space. Attempts would be made to monitor body temperature, chest movement and heart action, the latter by means of electrocardiograph. The required sensors must be comfortable and must not interfere with the astronaut's primary purpose.

At last the suiting was completed. Technician Joe W. Schmitt fitted hoses to the suits of the two astronauts in order to maintain comfortable temperature.

Astronaut Alan Shepard left the hangar carrying an air conditioner to cool his space suit until he could be hooked up to the cooling system in his capsule. He stepped into the transport van for the 3-mile trip.

At 0614 (6:14 A.M.) he stepped out of the van and headed toward the gantry and his ascent, by elevator, to his spaceship, *Freedom 7*. At 0620 (6:20 A.M.) he climbed into his capsule.

The launch team aimed for a firing at 0800 (8 A.M.). Eight o'clock came and went. Commander Shepard waited.

The team in the blockhouse waited.

Dee frowned as she looked around the room. If it was hard waiting here at the Forward Medical Station, how much harder it must be for the astronaut to wait inside the space capsule, not sure even yet if the launch would take place. Once before, the astronaut had almost blasted off. Could Al Shepard accept another false start and be calm enough to try again?

Was the delay causing psychological difficulties for the astronaut in his solitary quarters? The flight surgeon checked his monitoring devices. "Looks as if Al's the least nervous man of the bunch," he remarked.

So far so good . . . provided the launch came off. Commander Shepard was still in excellent condition. He'd have to be. If he could successfully leave the launch pad, he'd experience six times the force of grav-

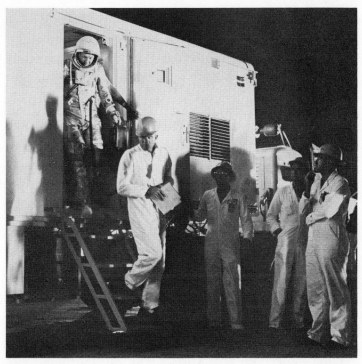

Eyes of the world focused on the spaceman as he stepped from van that transported him from Hangar S to launch site

ity during his climb. Then he'd have five minutes without any gravity at all, in the weightless period. On his abrupt re-entry—still assuming he had suffered no mishaps—he would be pressed into his couch with more than 7–8 times the force of gravity. What effects would these experiences have on the astronaut?

In her own mind, Dee ran over the list of adverse effects that had been considered.

13

Time dragged...0930 (9:30 A.M.).

"Sort of scary, isn't it?" Shirley asked.

Time was going too fast, somehow. Was it really worth the risk? How much real risk was there, anyway? Hadn't every conceivable precaution been taken? Hadn't each one of the astronauts undergone simulated space flights, been tested in conditions as close to the real ones as humanly possible? Hadn't they all come through with flying colors?

"How do you feel?" someone asked Dee.

How did she feel? Positive of the courage and ability of the man up there. Perhaps a bit annoyed at the hundreds of newsmen and cameramen swarming over the area. They acted as if a show were being staged for them. But perhaps in a way, they too were part of Mercury. Wasn't their purpose to bring the second-by-second story to the waiting world?

Ten thirty (1030). The final phase of the countdown. Five, four, three . . .

"Looks like this is *it*," someone said softly.

Two . . . one . . .

Zero. The time was 1034 (10:34 A.M.) Eastern Daylight Time. The date was 5 May, 1961.

The nurse's pulse raced.

A jet of yellow flame poured out and lifted the slender rocket off the pad. The medical support team in the blockhouse watched, awed. Thousands of persons who had worked for millions of man-hours watched. Around the world millions more watched. They stared at TV screens at home. They crowded into railroad stations to watch giant screens.

In seclusion, another friend of Dee's, Louise Shepard, watched. And no doubt prayed. With her were prayers of untold numbers. All Americans prayed, each in his own way, for the safety of one courageous man. Each felt a personal concern for him.

"All systems go. Everything okay," Alan Shepard reported. Calmly, methodically, he was recounting every detail of his historic flight by radio.

Then suddenly the calm gave way to excitement, to exhilaration, to sheer exultation as he saw the Eastern Coast of the United States from an altitude of 115 miles. *"What a view!"*

Soon now, the most critical phase of all was to come—re-entry into the earth's atmosphere.

The recovery fleet waited offshore. The carrier *Champlain,* six destroyers, and an assortment of search planes were standing by.

"Coming in for a landing," Astronaut Shepard said, as matter of factly as if returning from a routine training flight.

The time was 1049 (10:49 A.M.). The capsule hit the water some 302 miles out at sea, fifteen minutes and twenty-two seconds after launching.

Splashing into the sea, Mercury capsule makes its historic landing

Chapter 2
RECOVERY

Astronaut Alan Shepard had landed. The news flashed around the world. The world heaved a collective sigh of relief. Wasn't it only a matter of retrieving the capsule, now?

The medical support team in the blockhouse at Cape Canaveral knew better. It wasn't that simple.

The team in the blockhouse knew the normal reactions of the astronaut. And if there were an emergency situation, they would be flown to the recovery area.

Other precautions had been taken, as well. A surgeon, an anesthesiologist, and a group of medical technicians had been stationed aboard each destroyer. Each such team possessed a complete medical chest, for use in evaluation or for medical or surgical care.

These secondary teams would, if necessary, give

resuscitative care, then evacuate Commander Shepard to the nearest carrier. A carrier stood by in the Atlantic, set up for full-scale surgical procedures.

In advance of the flight, blood had been taken from donors, after typing and cross matching. Now, blood of Shepard's type was ready for transfusing, both at the Cape and at the recovery area.

A helicopter was ready to transport pararescue personnel, equipped with scuba diving gear, and a flight surgeon. The pararescue medical technicians were prepared to give first aid as well as to attempt a swimming rescue. Still other medical technicians were standing by on a small boat on the Banana River, ready to rush to the landing area in case of an abort or any other emergency.

Astronaut Shepard had the choice of remaining in his capsule and being lifted in it to the carrier deck, or of evacuating. He elected to leave his craft and wait to be picked up. A short time later he was lifted from his raft to a Marine helicopter.

"Thank you very much," he said courteously ... as if every day in the week he dropped from space and, on landing, simply waited a few minutes for a taxi to show up.

Then the infectious Shepard grin spread across his face. He looked around in wonder. "It's a beautiful day," he said fervently.

This was not a man waiting for a taxi after all.

This was the first American ever to have flown through space—and he was mighty glad to be back on earth.

And back at Cape Canaveral, someone asked of Dee O'Hara, "Now how do you feel?"

Elated. Ready to burst into tears, with sudden release from tension. Alan Shepard seemed to be as healthy as when he had entered his capsule. It wasn't over yet, of course, but it looked mighty fine from where Dee O'Hara stood. The astronaut would be flown to a rest area, debriefed, tested and so on, but the first indications were very encouraging—so far the space flight was a huge success.

"Isn't he great?" she answered. "He's one of the best."

Every reporter was bent on getting his human-interest story. Every person who had had any association with the astronaut was sought out to be interviewed. Dee was a prime target because she had spent one and a half years working in direct contact—with and for—the new space hero.

"What does it feel like to be part of the team?"

"What's he like as a person?"

"Don't you feel proud of yourself?"

Dee O'Hara was entitled to pride, but she was specific. "I'm proud of him, proud that I had the opportunity to do my part. But get this straight—Commander Shepard himself would be the first to point out that this was a team effort. A lot of people worked

To no one on the Mercury team did a safe landing mean more than to the nurse who had worked so long with the astronauts

very hard for a long, long time on Project Mercury. It's not just a one-man show. It's teamwork—and I'm proud of everyone on the team."

"How did you feel during those fifteen minutes when he was up there?"

"They were the longest fifteen minutes of my whole life," she admitted.

"How did you get the job as nurse for the astronauts?" someone else asked.

A good question. How indeed? She didn't answer

right then. The answer was too complicated—and too amazing.

A man with a camera demanded her attention. "With the name O'Hara, you must be Irish. If you're Irish, you must be a good Catholic girl," he said. "I heard you said the Rosary during the flight. Have you got it with you? Stand over here, Irish, and let me get a shot of you holding your Rosary."

Dee gave him an icy stare and stalked off.

It's newsmen like that who give all reporters a bad name, she thought furiously. Most of them are actually pretty decent. Oh, sure, once in a while they bugged the Project Mercury people, but they didn't do it on purpose. They certainly didn't mean to cause a commotion and perhaps endanger the astronauts. On the whole, they're okay. They try to be cooperative. They're doing a job and doing it well. They're the ones who make it possible for each citizen to keep informed on advances—as every person *should* keep informed.

Straight, factual, honest reporting is fine, she thought. It's a weapon against ignorance and fear. But this kind of thing—!

Forget it, she told herself. It's not worth bothering about, not today—not when America's first astronaut has been launched into space.

It was hard to believe it was real, even harder to believe that she, Dee O'Hara, had worked on the project from the beginning.

Cape Canaveral was a mighty long distance from Nampa, Idaho, population 16,000, where Dee was born on August 9, 1935. How in the wide world had she managed to wind up here at the Cape? Even more astonishing, how had she come to be a nurse to the astronauts? The first and *only* aerospace nurse.

"To go back to that question the reporter asked me," Dee thought, "how *did* I get the job? There is no simple answer to that one!"

Dee was the second child of Edward and Genevieve O'Hara. Bill, her brother, is a year older. It was a nice family. Average.

Dee might insist that *she* is average, but she never considered her father average. He was about 5 feet 10 inches tall—and he might as well have been 10 feet tall. He was her idol. He had the Irish black wavy hair and blue eyes, and he answered to the name of "Mick." A man of love, laughter, and a zest for life.

She didn't consider her mother, Jenny, average either. Jenny O'Hara was about 5 feet 5 inches tall, possessed of an adventurous spirit. And a special kind of strength—strength that they would all need, to sustain them, sooner than anyone realized.

And her brother Bill? He grew to 6 feet, eventually. Since he was only a year older, Bill and Dee had much in common and were good companions.

The family moved to San Francisco when Dee was 4 years old. Mick O'Hara went to work for

Bethlehem Steel Company. It was an experience in city living. San Francisco had its assets—a beautiful place, the chief seaport on the Pacific Coast. Sparkling white buildings reach up high hills. Trees line the walks with beds of vivid flowers growing around their bases. Clean, colorful. Romantic. But a city nonetheless. But Mick O'Hara wasn't a city man. He missed the wild splendors of Idaho.

The family moved again, this time to Crabtree, Oregon, population 500. This was a really small town, but Mick was happy. He went to work as a lumberman, outdoors.

Dee, Bill, and their friends had a type of freedom that youngsters have all too seldom. They swiped watermelons and had to run for their lives from their pursuers. Just normal kids—not delinquents.

A favorite haunt was the swimming hole. In season, they picked beans and strawberries. Not because they relished the thought of picking beans or strawberries. They didn't. But that's what youngsters did to earn money.

The fun they had was natural and imaginative, not bought in a package or labeled "educational." For instance, there was that wonderful Halloween party. It was staged by the grown-ups, undoubtedly under the leadership of one Mick O'Hara, who was at the top of the ladder when it came to imagination.

The night was dark and spooky when the young-

Dee graduated from Lebanon, Oregon, High School. It was here, during a "Career Day," she decided to become a nurse

sters arrived at the meeting place, an old barn and house. Outside were fresh graves, complete with tombstones. Most of them were covered with earth. But not all of them. Three or four were open, waiting. And, as if on cue, one 12-year-old boy fell in. Scared him half out of his wits!

White-robed ghosts flitted in and out among the markers, wailing eerily. And what was that huge, hulking monster lurking at the door to the barn?

A scream pierced the blackness. "It's a gorilla!" shrieked one of the girls.

It was the biggest gorilla in history. He was standing up on his hind legs, rattling a big chain held in his paw. Ready to pounce, he growled ferociously.

It was Mick O'Hara, dressed in an old fur coat, wearing a mask . . . but no one knew that. The children saw a gorilla—made real by imagination.

They got past the monster, miraculously, without a single casualty. Once inside, they crept up the creaky stairs. Horrors! There was a huge, black caldron bubbling away. A witch's caldron.

It was a Halloween party to be remembered.

But childhood comes to an end. It was time for Dee to begin high school. And then her troubles started. There was no high school in Crabtree, and she had to ride a school bus to a neighboring town.

For the first time in her life, Dee discovered that there can be a caste system among teen-agers. Boys and girls who lived in town and walked to school looked down on the bus kids.

The chief thorn in Dee's side was a girl named Jan McInnis. Jan lived in town. She was the same height as Dee—5 feet 6—but Jan had beautiful auburn *curly* hair, worn short. Dee's straight hair was done in pigtails, pinned on top of her head. Jan was . . .

"Stuck up."

"Sour puss," Jan retorted.

It was instant dislike, continuing dislike.

For two miserable years, Dee put up with the school. Then she got her Irish up and announced she wasn't going back. Ever. If she couldn't transfer to another school, ride another bus and hope for a better reception in another town, she'd quit altogether.

The transfer was effected and it was a fortunate move. The last two years of high school were wonderful. Dee found her misplaced sense of humor and enjoyed life again.

She had no specific plans for after graduation. No, Dee O'Hara had *not* dreamed, all her life, of becoming a nurse. She hadn't even considered the possibility of becoming a nurse. All she knew was that she liked people. She wanted to do something worthwhile, something that would really provide help. She thought vaguely of social work.

Then a career guidance day was held in school. It was the turning point of her life.

One of the speakers was a Registered Nurse. She had come from Providence Hospital, Portland, Oregon. She talked enthusiastically about nursing as a career, of the rich satisfactions that come from being of service to persons in need.

That talk rang a bell. Dee applied for admission to Providence Hospital School of Nursing.

In due time she was summoned to the city, some hundred miles away, for her interview.

"Have you had chemistry?" the interviewing nun asked.

"No, Sister," Dee admitted.

"Have you had algebra?"

"No, Sister," Dee answered, her throat tightening slowly.

"Have you had Latin?"

Dee shrank lower in her chair. "No, Sister."

The nun looked at her levelly. "Well, my dear," she said, "exactly what subjects *have* you had, if any?"

When Dee went home, her spirits were at a low ebb. She had filled out her application papers, but in her heart she knew she had failed. She was back where she started, not knowing what to do with her life. Only now it was worse, because time was running out and graduation was just around the corner. Her grades and character were good—but could those two factors alone get her into nursing?

And then the world fell down on Dee.

There was a logging accident. A man had been crushed to death.

It *couldn't* be Mick O'Hara. Not her idol, her adored father. She wouldn't let it be her father.

But it was. Mick O'Hara was dead.

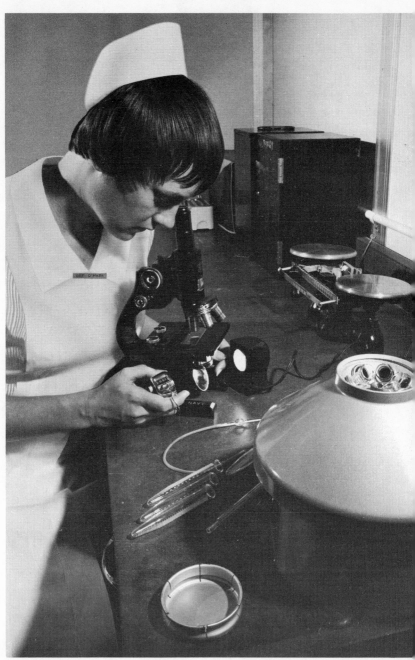

Laboratory procedures intrigued Dee from the beginning of her career

Chapter 3

STUDENT NURSE

Before her father's death, Dee had been torn between hoping for a letter from Providence Hospital School of Nursing and hoping no letter would ever arrive.

Now, with Mick O'Hara's death, it didn't seem to matter one way or the other. And sure enough, now that it was too late, the letter was here.

Dee hesitated, then ripped open the flap. Tears blurred her eyes so she could hardly read the message, but she saw she had been accepted. The impossible had happened . . . and yet it was equally impossible for her to leave home. The O'Haras, the three remaining O'Haras, had stuck together in their catastrophe. Dee wasn't going to walk out.

But it was worse, somehow, knowing that she'd had the chance. She fled to her room.

It was Jenny O'Hara who persuaded Dee to take the first step into what was to become a unique career.

"Your father never doubted that you'd be accepted," Mrs. O'Hara said. "And he never doubted that you'd become a nurse. Not just any old nurse, but the *best*. He had faith in you and he was proud you'd chosen this objective. You know he'd want you to—"

"What about you and Bill?" Dee asked. "It would be selfish of me—"

"You never had a selfish bone in your body," her mother answered. "As for Bill and me, we'll manage. You have been given an opportunity and a challenge and it's up to you to accept. Anyway, families can stay right in the same house and be separated by lack of love and understanding. The three of us are never going to lose our closeness, even if you go away."

So Dee began getting ready to go to Portland for three years. She looked forward to the experience with eagerness now that she was free of her guilt.

Then, before she left, her mother went shopping in town. "Guess what," she announced when she returned. "I ran into Jan McInnis' mother in one of the stores. Remember Jan?"

"Remember her?" Dee thought. "Only too well. The girl who made two years a misery."

"Well, it's quite a coincidence," Mrs. O'Hara went on, "but Jan's going to be a nurse too. She's even going to the same school, Providence."

"Oh *no*," Dee groaned.

"I'll bet you don't even remember what caused all the fuss," Mrs. O'Hara remarked shrewdly.

"I don't need to remember," retorted Dee. "I just know I can't stand her. If she's going to Providence, I'll go somewhere else."

It was late to register at another school. Besides, Jenny O'Hara was anxious for her daughter to attend a Catholic institution. Mostly out of consideration for her mother, Dee let the plans stand.

"I'll avoid Jan like the plague," Dee decided.

At last the fateful day dawned. Mrs. O'Hara drove Dee to Portland. As the miles slipped by, Dee's excitement mounted. She could hardly wait.

Then they turned into the drive. Dee stared at the tall, ten-story brick building. The first time she had seen it, her heart had lifted with hope. She had been sure this was where she wanted to be. Now her heart sank into her shoes.

"Let's go home," she said suddenly. "I've changed my mind."

Mrs. O'Hara kept driving. Dee felt as if she were riding in a tumbrel, on her way to the guillotine. And now it was too late. The car was parked and they were being swept along, bag and baggage, with girls and parents from all points.

The first thing to do was to go up the winding stairs, find her room, and get settled. On the way along

sheer physical stamina required of a professional nurse.

The days were filled with new and exciting adventures. There was so much to learn, and all of it was fascinating.

First there were orientation tours. The probies became familiar with the general layout of the hospital, the various departments—surgical, medical, obstetrics, pediatrics, out-patient. They sat in the gallery to observe surgical operations.

In class they began to learn basic laboratory procedures. They grew cultures, fixed slides, did urinalyses, discovered the various ways in which diseases could be transmitted.

The course in anatomy and physiology was intriguing. Before they learned about abnormal body structure and performance, they must know the normal. Dee and her classmates learned the name, shape, and placement of every bone in the human body. They learned the name, origin, and insertion of every muscle. They studied the nervous system, the circulatory system, the reproductive systems.

Procedures grew progressively more complicated as they went along. Soon they must know how to handle many intricate types of equipment.

The history of nursing gave them a greater insight into the background and value of their profession. Dee discovered that the Sisters of Charity, to which the nuns of Providence Hospital belonged, was

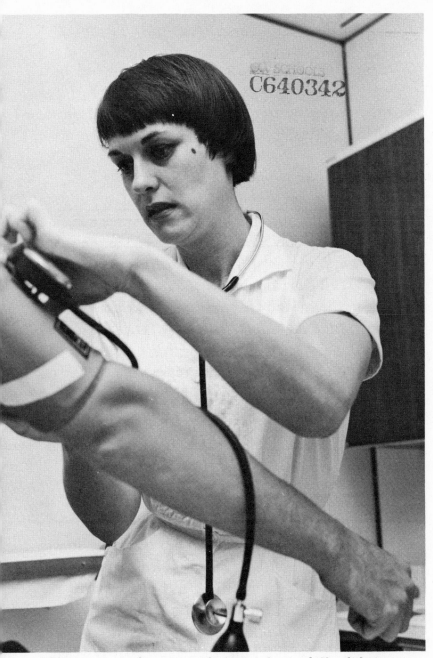

Never, as a student nurse learning basic skills, did Dee dream she would one day take an astronaut's blood pressure!

the oldest nursing order in the world. It had been established in 1634 by St. Vincent de Paul. And Dee drew inspiration from such nursing greats as Florence Nightingale and Clara Barton.

"I wish I could make a contribution, too," Dee thought. "Not for personal glory, but for *good.*"

If the days were filled with excitement, so were the nights. During off-duty hours there were initiation rites, varying only according to the vivid imaginations of the upperclassmen. There was never a dull minute.

With classwork by day and pranks by night, the students learned to take their careers seriously, but to take themselves less seriously. Woe betide the student who couldn't accept initiation with good grace!

After three months, the probies were allowed on ward duty. It was a bit unnerving, just at first, walking in among strangers and making the beds, taking temperatures, pulses, and respirations. But the strangeness soon wore off.

Just after Thanksgiving, a momentous announcement was made. "Each of you will be required to attend an autopsy."

The entire class buzzed with the news. It was scary. Imagine watching a human body being opened up. Imagine watching the organs being removed and examined!

"I bet I'll faint," someone whispered.

"Just remember that the human body is sacred,"

advised a nun. "We never handle it with anything but respect. But we use that body to gain knowledge."

Dee O'Hara faced a moment of truth. If she didn't attend the autopsy, she couldn't become a nurse. She came up with an answer that could well serve student nurses everywhere and change an ordeal into a privilege.

"It's—like opening a book," she said. "That's it. You open the book to gain knowledge."

The autopsy wasn't the least repulsive. Dee was intrigued. It really was a privilege to see what comprised a human body. It wasn't frightening; it was awe-inspiring. It was one of God's masterpieces.

At long last the great day—capping—arrived.

Parents and friends assembled in the auditorium. White bibs and aprons, over gray striped uniforms, rustled. The class filed in. Each girl carried a little lighted lamp, the symbol of the lamp Florence Nightingale used when she made her rounds among the soldiers injured at the Crimea, the lamp that has lighted the way for nurses ever since. Solemnly, the young girls knelt and bowed their bared heads.

This was the shining moment. The crisp white cap of Providence Hospital School of Nursing was placed on Dee's bent head, the cap traditional at Providence, with a miniature gold cross fastened to the left wing.

In her heart, Dee dedicated herself to nursing.

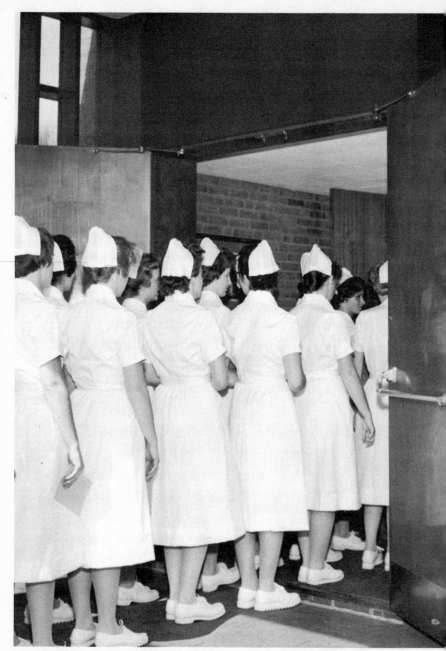

White uniforms at last! Proudly they filed in to their graduation

Chapter 4

THE PLEDGE

Life was quite different for Dee once she had her cap. She wore the symbol of her profession proudly, perched on her dark hair.

For, at last, Dee O'Hara looked like a real student nurse, exactly like any other student nurse. Her probie days were over. But she had barely scratched the surface of the vast store of knowledge she'd need to acquire before she'd be ready to assume real responsibility.

As the on-the-ward experiences became more interesting, so did the classwork. Now Dee and her friends really dug into obstetrics. They learned about the process of conception, gestation, and birth. Theory combined with practical experience and they all learned how to scrub to assist at a real delivery. Each felt the same awe when she held a brand-new baby, seconds old, and weighed it, measured it, and put the drops into its eyes. Lectures are all very well, but the reaction to that pint-sized person was "Look, it's alive!" Perfectly formed miniature hands with microscopic fingernails. Little fingers that could curl around a student nurse's forefinger with astonishing strength.

The operating-room tour really rang a bell for Dee. Here was real drama. A patient came in with something terribly wrong. Boldly, a surgeon corrected the trouble. Then the patient began to recover.

She really enjoyed learning to scrub her hands, wrists, and forearms—timing herself—to put on a sterile gown and gloves, and to set up an instrument table. It meant remembering which instruments were used for each type of operation. It even meant having a pretty good idea of the surgical procedure, because a scrub nurse should anticipate the surgeon's needs and have each instrument ready and waiting by the time he asks for it.

Life wasn't all work, of course, even though student nurses had far less free time than liberal-arts students in college. There were light moments on occasion—perhaps valued all the more because of their scarcity. There were dates with medical students from the University of Oregon, there were trips home. And there were occasional adventures and misadventures within the confines of Providence.

On one occasion, Dee lingered too long at a midnight supper in the hospital. Talking and kidding with the interns, she overstayed the time allowed her to get back inside the nurses' residence. The hospital was connected with the residence by a tunnel, but now the iron gate across that tunnel was closed and locked.

Dee groaned. "If I go out the front of the hospital and in the front of the nurses' residence, the House Mother will catch me. She'll skin me alive."

"Guess you haven't much choice," answered an intern sympathetically. "There's not much clearance between the top of the gate and the ceiling."

The student nurse eyed the gate speculatively. At the top were big spikes. But behind them, in the tunnel, they could hear footsteps approaching.

"Quick," she said, "boost me up. I'm going to try to squeeze through."

Scrambling up—the footsteps in the tunnel were coming closer—Dee almost made her escape. But her uniform caught on a spike. Being caught coming in late, by the front door, was one thing. Being caught dangling from a spike was a million times worse. Frantically ripping at the sturdy fabric, she freed herself in the nick of time. Clutching her tattered uniform, she scuttled to safety.

On-duty adventures were more solemn. Inevitably, the time came when Dee had to face the death of a patient. As a nurse, she had to learn that death, while the natural enemy, was a part of life, and that

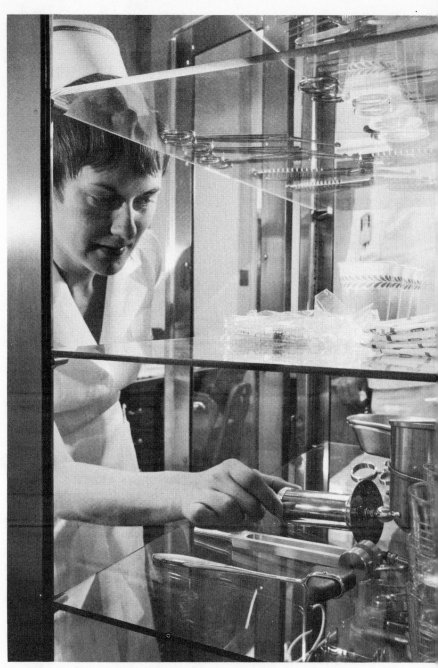

Row after row of shining instruments that must be checked—
Dee memorized their names, became familiar with their uses

while one life ended, over in the labor room, another life was beginning.

But the fact still remained that a body must be taken to the morgue. The job was given to Dee. She was told exactly where to place the body.

Inside the morgue was a refrigerator-like wall, with numbered drawers, each constructed with slats at the bottom. The trouble was, she couldn't remember which drawer she was to open.

Her mind was a blank, but she couldn't stay here all day. She yanked open a drawer quickly. Thank goodness! It was empty. Now she forced herself to lift her burden and place it, wrapped in its shroud, on the slats.

Then Dee made the mistake of looking down through the slats.

Staring up at her from the drawer below was an eye. A dark, unblinking, unwavering eye.

The hair stood up on the back of her neck. She stared back, hypnotized, rooted to the spot.

Then her good sense took over. How could this be? Whatever was down there should be covered with a shroud.

Finally her curiosity got the better of her. If she didn't find out the true story, she'd never be able to stop wondering. Taking a deep breath, she pulled open that drawer.

It was a rabbit. An inoffensive rabbit, placed

there for some future laboratory experiment. And now that she knew, Dee was free to scoot out on a dead run as if all the furies were in hot pursuit. Only—now there was no need to run. Strange—once you know the facts, fear evaporates. It's the fear of the unknown that's so terrifying.

By the time Dee reached the nurses' residence, her pulse was practically normal again.

It seemed as if everywhere that she turned there were things to pique Dee's curiosity. The more she learned, the more she realized she did not know— and the more she wanted to know.

She couldn't quite figure out how anyone could feel otherwise. Even the new group of probies. Good heavens, didn't they realize the privilege of learning?

She was totally sympathetic to the new ones, of course. And she remembered that initiation wasn't really always funny, not when carried to extremes. But she really laced them out when they complained of lack of freedom.

"We never have any fun," wailed one newcomer.

"I think maybe I'll quit while I'm ahead," said another.

Dee stared at the girl in chagrin. This probie seemed such a natural. Even her uniform was right for the tallish girl with short, naturally wavy dark brown hair and beautiful brown eyes. Her personality was warm and outgoing and she loved to tease. She wasn't teasing now, but Dee O'Hara wasn't going to let her miss the real satisfactions of good nursing.

"You listen here," Dee said bluntly. "Maybe you want to be a kid, now, but do you want to be a child all your life? In four years, the college kids will suddenly find that life is real—and they won't be ready to face up. Or maybe they'll never find out, and that would be worse.

"Which would you rather have? A scrapbook full of prom programs—or the chance to really help people?" Dee glanced around challengingly—and, in her heart, hopefully.

"Why not have the scrapbook and the career?" one of the girls wondered aloud. "Why not go to college and major in nursing? That way you have maybe two full years of college fun before you work in a hospital at all."

"Why be a nurse if you want to avoid working in a hospital?" Dee asked. "Sure, the college course would be fun. Two years of classes on some campus, dates, parties. You come out with a degree, having been educated to be a nurse-administrator or a nurse-teacher, but with less practical experience taking care of patients. Seems to me, aside from the extra cost of college, that you get more solid training in a school like Providence. Whoever said nursing was fun, anyway?"

Her eyes were wistful. College—yes, it would

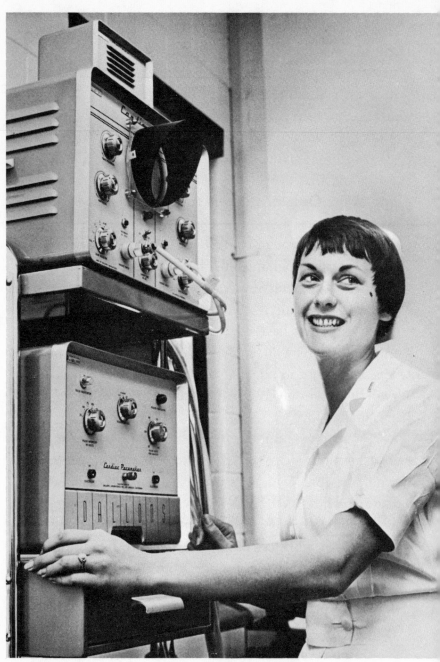

*Introduced to the electrocardiogram machine in student days,
Dee soon mastered its operation, learned to interpret results*

be easier and there would be fewer responsibilities. But there came a time when you had to make a choice —and grow up.

They got the message. Weeks later, after the probies were capped, they thanked Dee. She burst into tears, because they presented her with a poem saying that she'd shown them what nursing could mean.

Suddenly it was senior year for the class of 1956. Two thirds of Dee's training period was over—just like that. Each senior had the privilege of selecting the field in which she'd specialize. This was "Senior Rotation." Dee had elected operating-room technique.

Once again she discovered that the more she learned, the more intrigued she became and the more she wanted to know. If the first two years passed quickly, the third flew by like greased lightning. Sometimes she wanted to push against time, hold it back. It was all happening too soon. At the same time, she looked forward to the greatest thrill of all, the culmination of her basic training—graduation.

Unbelievably, it was the day. Never had there been such excitement as when some sixty girls, those who had survived the rigors of the past three years, put on their white uniforms for the first time.

They bounced in and out of each other's rooms, admiring their classmates and sneaking looks at themselves in every available mirror. They were as excited as probies waiting for their caps. But probies are so heartbreakingly young. These girls had eyes with new depths, for they knew about life—and death.

Once again parents and friends gathered in the auditorium. To the solemn tones of "Pomp and Circumstance," the members of the class of 1956 filed in.

There were speeches, reminders of the grave responsibilities each young graduate would assume, reminders that the completion of the course at Providence did not signify the end of the need to learn. A nurse must never stop learning. Each nurse must keep an open mind, an open heart, and a constant desire for more knowledge.

Each graduate received her cherished diploma and a rose corsage. Each received the distinctive pin she would wear on her uniform throughout her professional life, the pin designating her a graduate of Providence Hospital School of Nursing.

Now was the momentous occasion toward which they'd worked for three long years. It was time to rededicate themselves for all time to their profession.

Dee O'Hara looked down at the audience. She sought for and found the smiling woman whose blue eyes glistened with tears of pride. She glanced at Bill, her brother. For Dee it was the most wonderful moment of her life and yet there was an ache in her heart. If only Mick O'Hara were there! He'd wanted this for her; she'd wanted to justify his faith in her. Perhaps it had been the knowledge that she could never let him down that had helped her through to this chance to say the beautiful words of the Nightingale Pledge.

Her clear voice lifted with other young voices.

"I solemnly pledge myself before God and in the presence of this assembly, to pass my life in purity and to practice my profession faithfully.

"I will abstain from whatever is deleterious and mischievous and will not take or knowingly administer any harmful drug.

"I will do all in my power to maintain and elevate the standard of my profession and will hold in confidence all personal matters committed to my keeping, and all family affairs coming to my knowledge in the practice of my calling.

"With loyalty will I endeavor to aid the physician in his work and devote myself to the welfare of those committed to my care."

A hush followed the Pledge. Every new graduate, every member of the audience, felt the impact of that promise.

Then the tension snapped. Girls in white were embraced by families and friends. Laughter and tears mingled. But in the heart of each graduate was the big question.

"Am I able to meet these new responsibilities?"

Second Lieutenant Dee O'Hara, United States Air Force, Nurse Corps

Chapter 5

THE
OATH

Now it was Dee O'Hara facing the world on her own. Her immediate concern was State Boards, the formal examinations that followed graduation. Dee and Jan McInnis took the exams and passed the final hurdles. They now proudly designated themselves Registered Nurses. They were licensed to practice as such, and to wear pins to prove it.

The two girls moved out of Providence Hospital School of Nursing and into their own apartment. Dee now put in a full year at the University of Oregon learning operating room technique, and then she took a job as office nurse for three Portland doctors.

She had no way of knowing it at the time, but this was the second decisive step in her career. The decision to enter nursing had been the first step, but her first position as an R.N. put her in a different cate-

51

gory from her classmates and from graduates of other schools and universities.

During her years with the three doctors, she found great satisfaction in constant patient contact. Dee liked people and wanted to work directly with them. Now, in a very real sense, she gained every bit as much as she gave. What she received was intensive on-the-job training which would prove invaluable in her as yet undreamed of and completely unique future.

The office setup included a small pharmacy, so she learned a great deal about drugs. There was a minor surgery room and she learned to handle medical procedures above and beyond those of her hospital experience.

She learned laboratory procedures usually performed in hospitals by pathologists, by interns, by resident physicians. She learned blood typing and cross matching, various things few nurses know but things this particular nurse would eventually need to know. She went beyond the rudiments of electro-cardiography as learned in a hospital, and took over testing basal metabolic rates. She learned how to operate and monitor a myriad of machines that could tell the condition of a patient. She interpreted results.

Off duty, Jan and Dee had time to live a little. It was great fun learning to manage an apartment, to shop, to entertain at home. There were dates to add spice to their lives.

There was all of Portland to see, now that they had more freedom. The city is located in the northwestern part of the state on the Willamette River. It lies at the head of deep water navigation, only 14 miles from the place where the Columbia River and the Willamette converge, and a mere 113 miles from the Pacific Ocean. Mount Hood and other peaks of the Cascade Range are off to the east, some 40 miles.

Portland's place in the history of the country fascinated the girl who still had no idea that she, herself, would contribute to the history of her profession. The more the young nurse learned of Portland, the more she began to consider it her home.

One of the things she particularly loved was the annual Rose Festival. Portland is famous for its roses and its International Rose Test Gardens are located at Washington Park. Every June there was a week-long festival, with parades, banquets, and all sorts of festivities. People by the thousands thronged into the area.

And so that year passed, the first year of graduate duty for Dee O'Hara, R.N. and Jan McInnis, R.N. Then Jan left, to marry Ray Johnston.

It was a wrench for Dee. She contacted Jackie McMahan, a classmate of hers from Providence Hospital School of Nursing. The two had remained fast friends after graduation.

Jackie, a registered nurse herself, made her home with her family, there in Portland, and worked as a staff nurse at St. Vincent's Hospital.

"Mike"—somewhere along the way, her parents had re-nicknamed Jackie "Mike"—"how about moving into the apartment with me?" Dee asked.

Jackie demurred. "It would be silly. My folks live here in the city. Besides, I'm thinking of joining the Air Force Nurse Corps. Why move now, when I may be signing up any minute?"

"Come and try it," Dee urged. "Just for a week. See how you like it."

Jackie moved in on a temporary basis. And she stayed. At intervals, however, she brought up the Air Force Nurse Corps. She was restless and she communicated that restlessness to Dee.

By this time, office work had begun to pall for Dee. She had learned most of what there was to learn and that bump of curiosity was itching for more challenge. With things reduced to near-routine, it was time to move on and look at more of the world.

Perhaps it was the pouring rain that did it, that January day in 1959. Life seemed gloomy.

"Let's join the Air Force." It was Dee who said it this time.

The girls looked at each other. Each was calling the other, daring the other. Before they could lose their nerve, they phoned the recruiter and made an appointment to see him the following Tuesday.

Once they had filled out the necessary papers and

passed their physical exams, they were caught up in excitement.

"We'll have a chance to travel," they told each other gaily. "Just think, we'll work in all sorts of places, maybe overseas—"

"Commissioned officers—"

They didn't admit to each other that they were frightened. This was another step into the unknown, a little like applying for admission to Providence Hospital School of Nursing.

The two girls read eagerly all the literature provided by the recruiter, while waiting for their orders to come through. The requirements for acceptance had already been met. They were both citizens of the United States, between the ages of 20 and 35. They were physically fit. They were currently registered as professional nurses and they had been graduated from an accredited school of nursing offering no less than a three-year basic course. Neither had dependents under the age of 18.

They would be commissioned as second lieutenants since they held diplomas from a hospital school of nursing. A nurse holding a bachelor's degree could be commissioned as a first lieutenant. One with a master's degree could start as a captain. What Dee did not know was that by virtue of her extra on-the-job training and experience, she might well have received a higher rank. By the time she realized it, however,

Without accurate and detailed records, research projects would suffer. Dee gave full attention to those in her care

it was far too late for her to do anything about it.

"It says here that you can specialize," Jackie said, pointing to one of the pamphlets. "Obstetrics, anesthesiology, O.R. procedure, and administration. You going to ask for O.R.?"

"I think I'll put in for flight nursing," Dee answered, a far-off look in her eyes. "You can apply in about six months."

She read, for perhaps the hundredth time, the Flight Nurse's Creed.

"I will summon every resource to prevent the

triumph of death over life. I will stand guard over the medicines and equipment entrusted in my care and ensure their proper use . . . I have taken a nurse's oath reverent in man's mind because of the spirit and work of its creator, Florence Nightingale. She, I remember, was called the 'Lady With the Lamp.'

"It is now my privilege to lift this lamp of hope and faith and courage in my profession to heights not known by her in her time. Together with the help of flight surgeons and surgical technicians, I can set the skies ablaze with life and promise for the sick, injured, and wounded who are my sacred charges.

"This I will do. I will not falter in war or in peace."

At last their orders came through. The girls flew from Portland to Seattle, from Seattle to Chicago, from Chicago to Louisville, Kentucky. This was where nursing could lead; the sky was the limit and flying was the greatest. The plane broke down at Louisville, but not even that could dim their exuberance. What was a little old breakdown? Eventually they made it to Montgomery, Alabama, and then to Gunter Air Force Base. Here they would stay for a month of orientation. They were assigned six or eight to a room, with girls from all parts of the country.

Those first days were a little reminiscent of the first days at Providence, but on a larger scale. The girls were new and strange, but Dee soon made friends. Once again she was sure she had made the right decision, going into service. And the Air Force was the best branch of service.

There was another difference here at Gunter. In Providence they had waited to face an audience and solemnly dedicate themselves. In the Air Force they faced the American flag and took an oath. The words were solemn and awe-inspiring. They made you wish your parents were there. Jenny and Mick O'Hara. If only her father could watch—

"I, Dee O'Hara, having been appointed a second lieutenant in the United States Air Force Nurse Corps, do solemnly swear that I will support and defend the Constitution of the United States against all enemies, foreign and domestic; that I will bear true faith and allegiance to the same; that I take this obligation freely, without any mental reservation or purpose of evasion; and that I will well and faithfully discharge the duties of the office on which I am about to enter; so help me God."

What excitement there was when they received their uniforms! Not the once-coveted gray stripes, but a whole array. For street wear there were trim blue jackets and skirts, caps with white crowns and blue rolled brims with the Air Force insignia on the front. Crisp white jackets and skirts to be worn with white shirts and black neckties. Summer khakis of the same design. Seersuckers with short-sleeved jackets for hot weather. Hospital whites, and nurses' caps with light blue bands, each outfit better looking than the last.

And someday, Dee resolved, she would wear the flight-nurse uniform with the waist-length jacket, slacks, and the silver wings when she flew in a military aircraft.

In the meantime, it was enough of a thrill to wear second lieutenant's bars, and the caduceus, the winged staff that designated her a member of the Nurse Corps. WAF officers, women other than nurses, wore the same uniform but without the caduceus.

The days flew. As officers, the nurses must learn to march, to stand reviews and inspections just as in any military organization. They marched. And marched.

They learned military protocol. How and where and whom to salute. How to accept salutes. They learned about military courts of justice.

They learned the mission of the Air Force Medical Service: "To provide for the health needs of the Air Force population in both peace and war. It provides the medical support necessary to maintain the highest degree of combat readiness and effectiveness of the United States Air Force."

And they learned the fourfold mission of the Air Force Nurse Corps: "To provide the most efficient nursing care in a wide variety of specialties, not only in medicine and surgery at the bedside, but in the newest phase of airborne nursing at the litter in the plane. To teach patients and their families the principles of personal health. To teach and supervise nonprofessional personnel in nursing-care assignments in hospitals and as members of an air evacuation team. To participate in research activities toward the solution of problems in nursing."

That business of flight nursing really intrigued Dee. She read the history eagerly. It began in 1942, at Fort Benning, Georgia, with an air ambulance battalion. Two air evacuation units were sent overseas, one to the Pacific, the other to the Atlantic—with only two days of indoctrination.

The first actual course for flight nurses was conducted at Bowman Field, Kentucky, and was three weeks long. In addition to medical subjects, the nurses learned map reading, jeep driving, and marksmanship.

With the beginning of the Korean conflict, June 25, 1950, every available flight nurse was assigned to duty in the United States, the Pacific, or the Far East.

Since then, Air Force flight nurses have taken part in many rescue missions in flood areas and earthquakes. Huge evacuation jets now cross the Atlantic and Pacific twice a week, bringing home ill and wounded American servicemen and members of their families. The flight nurses train at Brooks Air Force Base, with its School of Aerospace Medicine.

This was for Dee, as soon as she was eligible.

Off duty as well as on, Dee enjoyed Gunter. There were swimming pools on base, craft shops, a gym. And Panama City was only about 150 miles away. Dee had a ball.

Then it was time for another graduation. This time nurses marched out to the field, to the accompaniment of a band. They heard about their new, grave responsibilities. They saluted.

"Officers dismissed!"

"Where are you and Jackie going to be stationed?" someone asked.

"Search me," Dee answered. "I haven't read my orders yet."

Her orders said Patrick Air Force Base, Florida. Jackie's said Mobile, Alabama. If they had only known, at the time they signed up, they could have requested assignment together. The Air Force makes every effort to honor such requests when friends join up together. Now it was too late.

Dee O'Hara was going to Patrick. Alone. Right near Cape Canaveral! She was on her own, facing the unknown. The young girl from Crabtree, Oregon, had come a long, long way. She had a long way to go.

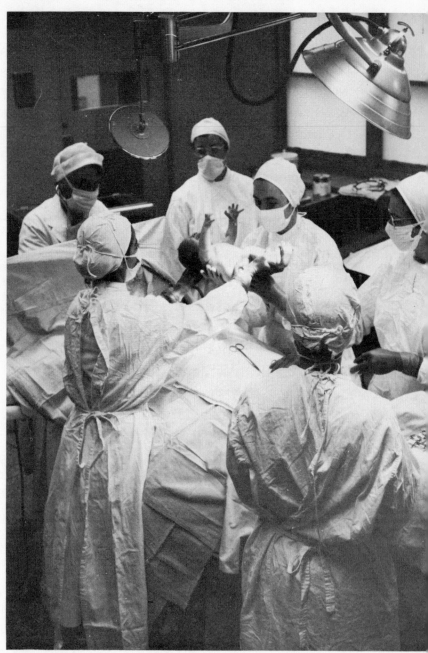

Dee took pleasure in helping at the ever-recurring miracle of birth

Chapter 6

COURT-MARTIAL?

Second Lieutenant Dee O'Hara, United States Air Force Nurse Corps, flew via Eastern Airlines from Montgomery, Alabama, to Melbourne, Florida.

She was alone on that trip, but in a sense she knew she would never be alone again. Not while she was in the Air Force.

In one short month at Gunter, she had discovered a surprising fact: A member of the military belongs to a vast family. Wherever he or she goes, there is always a bed, food, clothing, and medical and dental service available. Even if Dee were on leave, off in some strange corner of the earth, she need only go to the nearest Air Force facility and ask.

There would also be companionship in the military, because there is a close-knit loyalty within each branch. Many of the confusions and complications of civilian life are bypassed. Take travel, for instance. When on orders, transportation is provided. On leave, a member of the military, if in uniform, can travel at half fare.

So, although Dee O'Hara was physically alone as she stepped from the plane and into new adventure, she knew she would not be left to shift for herself.

She was met by her chief nurse, Major Margaret Price (now a lieutenant colonel), and Lieutenant Dotty Wilson, who took her to Patrick Air Force Base. Dee reported in, then went to see her new home, half of a duplex house in Wherry Housing.

Each duplex was shared by two nurses and consisted of two bedrooms, a living room, dining room, and kitchen. The kitchen, thanks to Major Mary Eckman, was already stocked with provisions in anticipation of Dee's arrival, and Dee was enchanted with this warm reception. She was going to love every moment at Patrick.

Or so she thought until she received her first assignment. Obstetrics.

Her heart sank. She hadn't had any O.B. work since training and she knew this would be no mere floor duty under supervision. This time *she* would be the supervisor.

She certainly hadn't signed up with the Air Force to work in O.B. She didn't know doolie about O.B., she reminded herself.

A "doolie" in Air Force lingo is a greenhorn. He's a first-year student in the Air Force Academy in Colorado Springs, a freshman.

"Put me in the operating room," she urged her superiors. "I know what I'm doing in the O.R."

A throat was cleared. An ever so slightly amused eyebrow was raised. "You're in the military. You wouldn't be assigned to a position you couldn't handle."

And a second lieutenant, if she really wants to be a credit to her branch of service, accepts orders, Dee knew. She accepts orders with good grace.

"Yes, Ma'am," said the second lieutenant. "O.B."

In her mind's eye she saw Providence Hospital, and a nun saying much the same thing. For the protection of the patient, no nurse without full qualifications would be given charge duties. Dee decided, again, to chalk it up to experience, refresh her memory, go on and learn everything possible and provide the best possible care. Her patients would be wives and infants of men in the Air Force, her branch of service. Nothing was too good for them.

There was a lot to remember even in a normal delivery. First of all, a nurse must fully understand the three steps of the phenomenon of labor, the process by which a child is born. During the first stage, the cervix or lower part of the uterus expands. In the second, the infant is expelled. And in the final stage the placenta, the tissue which is attached to the inside of the uterus during pregnancy and from which the infant receives his nourishment, is expelled.

A nurse must be able to count the fetal heartbeat during labor. With a special stethoscope, she must locate the unborn child's heartbeat through the mother's abdomen. It is important to keep checking that beat to make sure the baby remains in good condition.

During labor, Dee knew, a nurse could do many things to insure the safety and comfort of both mother and baby and to make the experience more pleasant. In a very literal sense, the nurse could prevent much or all of the pain associated with labor. Fear alone causes a great deal of that pain because, with fear, muscles contract and make the passage of the baby much more difficult.

"Breathe deeply," she'd advise a patient. "This will help ventilate you and relax your muscles. Relax between contractions and save your energy. But do think of them as contractions, rather than as pains. It helps to remember that birth is a normal, if miraculous, process."

A little O'Hara teasing often helped to lighten fears but, for those who needed it, there was ample O'Hara tenderness—and the old O'Hara enthusiasm for adventure, which she could communicate to a patient in labor.

"Can't wait to see whether it's a boy or a girl,

can you?" she'd ask, urging her patient to take an active part by bearing down during contractions.

It helped to keep the patient busy. It helped to focus on the job to be done and on the end result, rather than on the discomfort.

When the cervix was dilated, off they'd go to the delivery room. There was a baby to be coaxed into the world, perhaps head first, perhaps seat first, in what is known as the breech position.

Then there was a yell of outrage as the infant catapulted from his snug, warm berth of the past nine months out into the cold world. Such a furious little bundle of humanity!

There were drops to be put in the newcomer's eyes to prevent any possibility of infection, a foot-print to be recorded on the chart, along with the mother's fingerprint, for purposes of identification, weighing in, measuring. Then the wonderful new baby was snug and warm again, wrapped in a fluffy blanket, ready to be introduced to his proud parents.

O.B was never dull. Babies seem to pick the darndest times to appear.

But close to Patrick Air Force Base there was more excitement. Missiles were being launched at Capt Canaveral. In a way, Dee couldn't help envying the registered nurses attached to Pan American World Airways and now based at Patrick. Those the missile nurses and they were engaged in exciting and

Medical records of Project Mercury astronauts assumed vast importance. Dee was responsible for keeping them up to date

adventurous work that was right up Dee's alley.

Pan Am was under contract to the Air Force to operate the Atlantic Missile Range. The range reached from the Cape through the Bahamas, across the southern part of the Atlantic Ocean and across the southern part of Africa, terminating in the Indian Ocean.

Part of Pan Am's responsibility was medical support for all personnel engaged in missile work. The yearly patient volume was close to 100,000. There were six dispensaries within the United States, eleven radio-equipped ambulances, twenty-two nurses, ten medical orderlies, eight doctors, and several X-Ray technicians. Service was provided around the clock, seven days a week.

The missile nurses had not only the opportunity, but the necessity of becoming familiar with various rocket fuels, learning their physical properties and the ill effects they could cause. Since missilemen handle radioactive material, they had to learn how to measure radiation with Geiger counters, and how to care for patients exposed to radiation.

They knew how to use Scott Air Packs, self-contained breathing apparatus such as that used by firemen who must go through smoke or air contamination. They were familiar with gas masks. They might, in the event of a major accident, use any or all of that equipment and more.

The blast hazard was greatest following an impact—that is, when a missile returns to land anywhere between 100 and 1,000 feet from the launching pad. The Pan Am nurses stood by at every launch, ready for action in case of an explosion.

Every month they had a drill, during a simulated disaster. During the drills, disaster crews worked right along with them. Those crews were recruited from the workers themselves and were men who had taken a course of instruction similar to that given by the Red Cross for first-aid instructors.

In one such drill, a fuel mixture was exploded. The problem was how to take care of twenty simulated casualties and numerous hysterical bystanders. A forward field hospital was set up and nurses and disaster crews carried the uncontaminated "patients" by stretcher to the wards.

One "patient" was considered contaminated by radiation. His clothing was cut off and he was washed down with water from the fire truck. A nurse applied a splint to a leg that was supposedly fractured. Every phase of rescue work must be practiced and practiced, because if a real disaster occurred there would be no time to explain procedures. Everyone must be ready, at all times.

The now-decontaminated patient was carried to the field hospital, situated on the very edge of the disaster area. The hospital was set up with three wards, each designated by color. Red meant severe injuries, yellow, slightly less severe, and green indicated minor cases. A nurse was in charge of each ward. In the event of a real disaster, each nurse would keep her station operating, give immediate care to the injured, then evacuate the patients to nearby hospitals for more intensive medical and nursing care.

In many respects, the work of the Pan Am nurses seemed more like the military nursing of which Dee had dreamed than what she was doing at the hospital at Patrick Air Force Base.

Dee wanted challenge—challenge like that faced by a missile nurse who climbed out on a narrow beam, a good 234 feet above the ground, to help a worker who had lost consciousness up there. The nurse gave him first aid on the spot. Dee wanted the feeling that another nurse must have had when she gave first aid 50 feet below the surface of the ground to an employee who had been knocked unconscious in one of the underground launching sites.

"That's really living," Dee thought. "Look at all the patient contact. The Pan Am nurses rotate so they all get turns making those daily visits to the launch sites."

With so many thousands of workers, time out to visit a dispensary for treatment of minor ills would add up to a tremendous loss in time. Pan Am brought medical services to them on the job, instead. A nurse and a medical orderly made the circuit by ambulance.

First the nurse and medic would go to the main dispensary to pick up their supplies and be briefed. They'd be told what fueling or defueling was going on, so they'd know what toxic conditions were on the list of things to watch. They'd know where to check up to make sure all workers were using the necessary protective equipment or clothing. Part of their job— a large part—was the constant teaching of safety measures and accident prevention.

Then, equipped with their Scott Air Packs, gas

masks, and Geiger counters, they'd set off. With them went oxygen, splints, equipment for administering intravenous injections, and a kit used for treating minor injuries.

At each gate they'd be cleared by security guards and a public-address system would announce that the Pan Am nurse was ready to see patients. They averaged twenty to thirty minutes in each area, but they maintained radio contact with the main dispensary at all times. If an accident occurred elsewhere, they could get there in a hurry.

This was exciting work that was never routine. Not that Dee would give up the Air Force. Actually, she couldn't resign in less than the required two years of minimum duty, but it did seem to be mighty dramatic over there with the Pan Am gang.

"Oh well. Flight nursing would be even better," she told herself.

She had put in for flight nursing. She still had her sights set on those silver wings. Her orders might come through any day now ...

Only they didn't.

The only orders she received were relayed to her by her roommate, verbally.

"You are supposed to report to Colonel Veit."

Colonel John Veit was the deputy commander of the hospital at Patrick. Being summoned to his office gave Dee real qualms. It sounded as if she'd done something wrong. But what? She was shaking in her shoes when she reported.

"Shake a little harder," Colonel Veit said. "The Old Man wants to see you."

The Old Man, as anyone who has ever served in the military knows, is always the commanding officer. In this case he was Colonel George Knauf, hospital commander and Center staff surgeon.

Being summoned by Colonel Knauf had to mean one of two things. Promotion—or trouble.

And it wasn't time for Dee to be promoted.

It must be trouble. Awful trouble. Maybe even a court-martial!

When Dee went into Colonel Knauf's office there were only two persons there, the colonel and the chief nurse. It looked worse by the minute.

All Dee could think was "What have I done?"

Her mind was frozen. She didn't even notice the oddity, the informality, of the colonel's greeting.

"Sit down here, Dee," he said.

She sat. He talked but she hardly heard a word. Her mind was too busy scurrying around like a squirrel in a cage trying to figure out where and how she had goofed and how serious the offense might be.

The only word that registered was "Mercury."

"Know anything about it?" the colonel asked.

"All I know about mercury is that it's used in thermometers," she admitted. "Oh—and it's the name of one of the planets," she added after a moment.

"I'm talking about Project Mercury," he said, smothering a grin. "You know, the project that is to be conducted by the National Aeronautics and Space Administration to launch a manned spacecraft."

"Fine, but what does that have to do with me," Dee wondered.

"It's still in the organizing stages," the colonel went on. "It was actually instituted about a year ago. The purpose, as I said, is to put a man into space.

"Before that can be accomplished, there's a tremendous amount of work to be done. The millions of headaches concerning the spacecraft belong to the scientists and engineers. The concern of any medical personnel must be for the astronaut."

"Astronaut?" Dee O'Hara had no idea what the word meant.

"The pilot of the spacecraft. The man who will fly in space. The first team of astronauts will be selected in the spring."

He went on to tell about Project Mercury, briefly.

"How will NASA choose the team of astronauts?" Dee asked. "Will they be volunteers?"

In a sense, yes, she was told—no one would be assigned unless he were eager. Mere interest would not be enough. The selection board must find the very best men for the job. Each would be a test pilot, someone already accustomed to trying out new means of flying. He must possess superior skills in flying and he must be extremely stable, the type who could cope with the unexpected. Each must be well versed in engineering.

From a medical standpoint, each must be in near-perfect physical condition. He must be able to withstand great stress to both mind and body. There must be reasonable assurance that he would remain free of physical troubles during the entire project, for enormous amounts of time and money would be invested in him.

Dee still couldn't figure out what all this had to do with her. It was terribly exciting, of course, but . . . "Are you going to make the selections?"

No. Colonel Knauf would help select some of the medical team that would work with the astronauts.

The colonel paused, then added casually, "Dee, how would you like to be the nurse assigned to the astronauts?"

Dee's jaw dropped in a most unmilitary manner.

"The fellows"—the original astronauts—grouped around a capsule

Chapter 7

HANGARS

The girl with the pixie haircut stared at her commanding officer in astonishment. She could hardly believe her ears—or her good fortune.

When she'd first embarked on a career in nursing, she'd felt that the sky was the limit. Reaching toward that limit, she'd entered the Air Force Nurse Corps, hoping to become a flight nurse. Now, even if she didn't have those coveted silver wings, it looked as if the limit were far beyond the sky. There were no limits at all.

With effort, she brought her soaring imagination down to earth. Why would the astronauts need a nurse at all? They'd be practically supermen, the healthiest lot available. Much as she'd adore to be on the inside of Project Mercury, what on earth would there be for her to do? She couldn't sit around twiddling her thumbs on the off chance that an astronaut might become ill.

A nurse was supposed to take care of the sick and injured.

Yes, under ordinary circumstances, agreed the colonel. These circumstances, however, were far from ordinary.

"Usually we doctors and nurses care for abnormal—that is, sick—individuals in a normal environment—earth. In aerospace medicine we must learn to take care of normal individuals in a hostile environment—space."

That made sense. The customary task facing doctors and nurses was to restore a person to normal. In Project Mercury, the problem would be to keep him normal in situations which a human being was not designed to meet. Those situations were beyond Dee's wildest imaginings.

"Will *I* be expected to fly in space?"

At present, she learned, there were no plans for putting a nurse in space. The purpose of Project Mercury was to launch healthy men, one at a time, for short periods. In later years, there would be a Project Gemini, to try to launch two-man teams in space. A Project Apollo would follow to try to put three-man teams in space and eventually land two men on the moon.

"How about it?" prompted Colonel Knauf.

"Yes, Sir," she answered promptly. Affirmative. Positively. "But why me?"

Colonel Knauf had personally selected Dee O'Hara. She had an enthusiasm for adventure and a stability to handle the always necessary routine work. Her warm, outgoing personality was what was needed, the colonel had decided, to get along with men who would be somewhat separated from the world and who, facing the unknown, would be under great tension.

She had, he felt, the ability to dedicate herself to the group, without playing favorites. She had the vital ability to stand quite a bit of isolation herself, would be able to work under stress, and still keep the emotional climate calm and pleasant for the astronauts. A temperamental nurse could have spelled disaster.

Why look farther, Colonel Knauf reasoned. There wasn't time to train a nurse in the things Dee already knew. She could perform many lab procedures. She could slide a needle into a vein and withdraw blood samples for typing and cross matching. She could operate many complicated machines used to test body reactions and she could interpret the results of such tests.

She was a natural and she was *there.* She was at the right place at the right time, with a record that spoke for her.

When she left Colonel Knauf's office, Dee felt

positively dazed. The whole thing was so improbable!

Imagine having to keep such news to herself! Go on duty but keep the news under her hat until an official statement was made. On the other hand, she wasn't anxious to have the news given out at all. She was only a second lieutenant. Many of her friends in the Nurse Corps outranked her. Wouldn't they be hurt and perhaps even justifiably angry? She wouldn't want that—

If Dee had but known, there was one serious threat to her appointment, although Colonel Knauf was sticking to his guns.

Back she went, on night duty, at Patrick Air Force Base Hospital. Inwardly bursting with excitement, she was outwardly the same Dee O'Hara.

What she didn't know didn't bother her. She had two major concerns: to do the best possible job and to avoid hurting her friends. She really worried about the latter.

During the days, she often had to forgo sleep because Colonel Knauf summoned her to accompany him on various trips. They covered many miles by air and attended many meetings.

Dee found out quite a bit later that the colonel had used this means to accustom her to constant air travel. As time went on and Project Mercury progressed, part of her job consisted of traveling alone on speaking engagements.

She devoted a part of her time, for a long while, to such lectures. She addressed groups of nurses at district meetings, spoke to university groups, assisted in recruiting programs. Her task in this area was to explain developments in the new field of aerospace nursing.

What with night duty and traveling, her dual role began to take a toll. Her vivacity wore a bit thin, but the stubborn Irish in her refused to stoop to complaining. As it turned out, the colonel put an end to her fatigue by having her relieved of all hospital duties.

Now she was on loan, full time, to NASA. And now the news was out. An aerospace nurse had been appointed for Project Mercury.

Her many friends in the Nurse Corps were genuinely happy for her good fortune—the first aerospace nurse. But newsmen now sought her out. She couldn't avoid them because part of her job was to acquaint the public with her part in the project, but she kept stumbling over problems.

"Space Nurse," the newsmen dubbed her. "Astronaut Nurse," others cried in print.

"Both titles are absolutely incorrect," she pointed out. "The only proper designation is aerospace nurse—a nurse, stationed on earth, who is working with men who travel in air and space. I'm not a nurse who travels or works in space. There's a difference."

She had her troubles with writers who wanted to exalt her, make her a heroine.

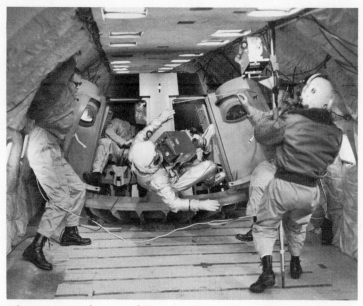

Floating in the weightless state of zero gravity was part of the training all Project Mercury astronauts underwent

"I'm just an ordinary nurse," she insisted. "It's the *job* that's extraordinary."

There was no denying, though, that her life was going to be varied and exciting enough to satisfy even a Dee O'Hara.

To add to the enjoyment, Lieutenant Shirley Sineath, with whom Dee shared a duplex, was assigned to a facet of Project Mercury. Shirley was put in charge of all medical kits, supplies, and equipment to be shipped down-range, around the world, in case such supplies might be needed during a flight. This was a full-time, Herculean task because she managed some 32,000 individual sets of sterile items packed into the various kits.

It was true that only Dee would work in close contact with the astronauts, but the girls could share a common interest in the over-all effort.

The seven astronauts for Project Mercury were selected in April of 1959. They were Alan B. Shepard Jr., Virgil I. Grissom, John H. Glenn Jr., M. Scott Carpenter, Walter M. Schirra Jr., L. Gordon Cooper Jr., and Donald K. Slayton.

Dee didn't meet them right away. There were no permanent facilities at the Cape for their training. They underwent various phases of training in several places.

At Langley Field, Virginia, they had a fifty-four hour course in astronautics, given by NASA. The McDonnell Engineering Corporation gave them lectures on Project Mercury sub-systems and on code training. Dr. William K. Douglas, their personal physician, explained the problems of space flight from the aeromedical standpoint.

The famous seven took a concentrated course in star recognition and celestial navigation at Chapel Hill, North Carolina, at the Morehead Planetarium. They underwent a five-and-a-half-day course in desert survival at Stead Air Force Base, Nevada, on the chance that they might land on some desert area such as Africa's Sahara after their various flights.

They rehearsed in the Navy centrifuge at Johnsville, Pennsylvania, and in a specially designed altitude chamber in the famous Hangar S at Cape Canaveral later on.

Dee followed news of them avidly. These would be her charges. It was up to her to know everything possible about them. She'd be responsible for keeping their medical records and, in order to spot any abnormality, she'd have to know what was normal for each.

She and Shirley went over the basic biographies of the group, their eyes almost rolling right out of their heads.

Lieutenant Commander Shepard Jr., U.S.N., was a native of East Derry, New Hampshire, according to the records. He had been graduated from the United States Naval Academy, Annapolis, in 1944 and from the Naval War College, Newport, Rhode Island, in 1958.

He attended the Navy Test Pilot School, Patuxent River, Maryland, and served two tours of duty there. He took part in high altitude tests, in the development of in-flight refueling, in landing trials of the first angled carrier deck. He tested such aircraft as the F2H3 Banshee, the F3H Demon, the F8U Crusader, the F4D Skyray, the F11F Tigercat, and the F5D Skylancer. He served as an instructor at the Test Pilot School for five months.

He was married to the former Louise Brewer of

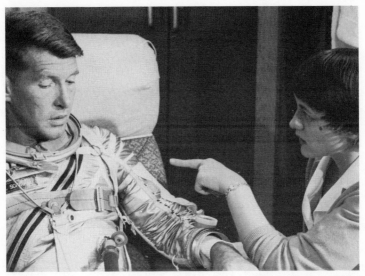

Suited up for a simulated orbital mission, astronaut Walter Schirra talked over medical aspects of the flight with Dee

Kennett Square, Pennsylvania. The couple had two daughters, Juliana and Laura.

Virgil "Gus" Grissom was an Air Force captain. He received a bachelor's degree in mechanical engineering from Purdue University in 1950, won his wings in 1951, and flew 100 combat missions in Korea. He served as a jet pilot instructor at Bryan, Texas.

He studied aeronautical engineering at the Air Force Institute of Technology, Wright-Patterson AFB, Ohio, then attended Test Pilot School at Edwards AFB, California. Returning to Wright-Patterson, he was assigned as a test pilot in the Fighter Branch.

He married Betty L. Moore of Mitchell, Indiana. The couple had two sons Scott and Mark.

John Glenn, a Marine Corps lieutenant colonel, was born in Cambridge, Ohio. He attended Muskingum College, took part in the Naval Aviation Cadet program and attended the University of Maryland.

He flew 59 combat missions during World War II with Marine Fighter Squadron 155 in the Pacific theater. He flew 63 missions during the Korean conflict with Marine Fighter Squadron 311 and another 27 with the Air Force, as an exchange pilot.

He attended Test Pilot School at Patuxent River, served as project officer on several aircraft, and then was assigned to the Navy Bureau of Aeronautics in Washington, D.C., in the Fighter Design Branch.

His decorations included the Distinguished Flying Cross, awarded five times, and the Air Medal with eighteen clusters. On top of all that, he set a transcontinental flight record from Los Angeles to New York: three hours twenty-five minutes in an F8U.

Glenn's wife was the former Ann Margaret Castor of New Concord, Ohio. The Glenns were the parents of two children, John David and Carolyn Ann.

Scott Carpenter, a lieutenant in the Navy, was born in Boulder, Colorado. He attended Colorado College under the Navy's V-5 program, then trained at St. Mary's Pre-Flight School, Morago, California, and at Ottumwa, Iowa. At the close of World War II, he attended the University of Colorado, Boulder, and took Navy flight training in 1949.

During the Korean action he took part in anti-submarine shipping surveillance and aerial mining activities with Patrol Squadron 6, in the Yellow Sea, the South China Sea, and the Formosa Strait. He, too, attended Navy Test Pilot School and was subsequently assigned to the Electronics Test Division.

His wife was the former Rene Louise Price of Boulder. Their children were Marc, Jay, Kristen, and Candace.

Walter Schirra Jr. was a Navy lieutenant commander. He was born in Hackensack, New Jersey, and had a year at the Newark College of Engineering before being appointed to the Naval Academy. After his graduation in 1945, he was ordered to Pensacola for flight training, then served with Fighter Squadron 71. He flew 90 missions in Korea as an exchange pilot with the Air Force. He received the Distinguished Flying Cross with two Air Medals.

Schirra had a hand in the development of the Sidewinder missile, was project pilot for the F7U Cutlass, and was an instructor for both the Cutlass and the FJ3 Fury. He attended Naval Air Safety Officers School at the University of Southern California and Test Pilot School at Patuxent River.

He, like all the others, was married. He and his

wife, the former Josephine C. Fraser of Seattle, Washington, had two children, Walter III and Suzanne.

Gordon Cooper, a captain in the Air Force, was born in Shawnee, Oklahoma. His career was so varied that it almost defied belief.

He served in the Marine Corps, then attended the Naval Academy Preparatory School at Bainbridge, Maryland. He then became a member of the Presidential Honor Guard in Washington, D.C. He attended the University of Hawaii and received an Army commission. Then he transferred to the Air Force and was ordered to flight training in 1949.

Captain Cooper attended the European Extension of the University of Maryland and the Air Force Institute of Technology and earned a bachelor's degree in aeronautical engineering. He then attended the Air Force Experimental Flight Test School, Edwards AFB. After graduation he was assigned to the Performance Engineering Branch of the Flight Test Division.

He married Trudy Olson of Seattle, Washington. The couple had two daughters, Camala and Janita.

Donald "Deke" Slayton, an Air Force captain, was born in Sparta, Wisconsin. He received a bachelor's degree in aeronautical engineering from the University of Minnesota in 1949. He had previously won his wings in 1942.

He flew 56 combat missions with the 304th

Bombardment Group in Okinawa, seven combat missions over Japan, and spent another year as an instructor. He then entered the University of Minnesota and, after graduation, did a stint with Boeing Aircraft Company as an aeronautics engineer.

Slayton returned to active duty with the Minnesota National Guard. After attending Test Pilot School at Edwards AFB, he spent three years as an experimental jet aircraft pilot.

He married Marjorie Lunney of Los Angeles. The couple had one son, Kent.

These were the astronauts, the cream of the crop. The best men that could be found for Project Mercury. What, in heaven's name, was the girl from Crabtree, Oregon, population 500, going to do in a group like that?

"What a load of talent," Dee whistled.

She threw herself into the next phase of her work. Dee O'Hara was responsible for setting up the astronauts' area on the second floor of Hanger S, early in 1960. The hangar was located directly on the Cape, about 12 miles north of Patrick.

Dee met her first astronaut quite by chance, when she was on tour of the area. To her relief, Deke Slayton was a regular human being. Not a wheeler-dealer at all, in spite of his phenomenal record.

She met the group itself by mistake. She didn't even know they were there, in Hangar S, when she opened the door of the conference room without a second thought.

"Ooops, sorry," she apologized, backing out hastily.

"Hey, come on back," laughed Deke Slayton. "Come and meet the fellows."

He introduced everyone and, from then on, they were "the fellows" to the girl from Crabtree. And she was "Dee" to them, to their wives and children.

Dee's qualms about working with such an illustrious group simply flew out the window. She slid easily into her role of nurse to the astronauts, big sister, kid sister, protector of their privacy, friend of their families.

Hangar S was home base, where the girl from Oregon put to use all her unique training—the basic education acquired at Providence, the advanced training with the Portland internists and diagnosticians.

She hadn't known in advance where her profession would lead her. She hadn't known that there would be a need for an aerospace nurse, any more than the astronauts necessarily knew the time was ripe for manned space flights. But she was prepared as completely as possible, just as they were prepared.

Dee played it by ear, for there were no textbooks for reference. She took the course given at the Cape for aerospace surgeons and figured things out as she went along—paving the way for future nurses.

An "ordinary person," she termed herself. She was simply a nurse with an extraordinary job, a girl who traveled all over the country giving speeches, meeting all sorts of famous persons, and then went back to Hangar S to work with the seven astronauts on whom the eyes of the world were focused—a girl who was destined, through circumstances, to become famous herself.

Dee O'Hara was a nurse who could have missed out on the chance of a lifetime, just as one of the astronauts could have missed out on his chance.

Special equipment enabled Cooper to monitor his own blood pressure

Chapter 8

MEN IN SPACE

Alan Shepard thought he was missing the big chance. Apparently he had the qualifications to become an astronaut but he lacked a vital piece of paper, the notice of acceptance. Fortunately it had merely been delayed in the mail.

Another astronaut might have been disqualified for lack of a piece of paper. Scott Carpenter was obviously qualified, through theoretical and practical work, for the enormous task ahead. Fortunately, his lack of a formal college degree was bypassed. It was a mere technicality.

In the case of Dee O'Hara, the lack of a college degree could have barred her. When it was time to appoint the first aerospace nurse, the officials in the Nurse Corps quite understandably thought in terms of a college degree. Such a nurse would need a tremendous store of technological knowledge, of the type not taught in the kind of diploma course Dee had taken at the Providence School of Nursing.

Fortunately, the rule-in-the-making was waived when Colonel Knauf pointed out Dee's qualifications. Just a degree, any degree, wouldn't automatically make a nurse ready for the job. Just as any degree, even in engineering, wouldn't automatically qualify a pilot as much as Scott Carpenter had qualified himself for his part in Project Mercury.

Recognition of Dee's unique training resulted in her appointment. She had earned the right to be the first aerospace nurse and to be in the blockhouse that fateful day of 5 May, 1961. She was part of the medical team. With the team, she sweated out the hours, praying for the safe recovery of Alan Shepard and breathing a sigh of relief when the news came.

Then it was time to go through it all again. This time it was Gus Grissom. The date was 21 July, 1961. In his silver nylon space suit, he entered the capsule *Liberty Bell* 7, at 0438 (4:38 A.M.). Preparations were a bit hurried, for a storm was forming in the Caribbean, near the landing site. He was launched at 0820 (8:20 A.M.). Within the next thirty minutes he was to float in two different elements.

Once again the world watched and prayed. Once again the group in the blockhouse monitored his condition and waited, fighting personal inner tensions.

94

The *Liberty Bell* 7 landed at 0836 (8:36 A.M.), 303 miles from the Cape. It looked like another total success. But wait . . .

One minute the astronaut was communicating with the crew of the rescue helicopter, and the next instant, for reasons that could not be determined, the escape hatch blew from the side of the capsule. Sea water surged in.

Now the pilot had no choice. Until the hatch blew, it was up to him to decide whether he'd climb out and wait for his pickup, riding in his raft, or wait to be picked up inside the capsule. The choice was taken out of his hands. He climbed out.

To the team in the blockhouse, the concern was for the life of the pilot. It was of secondary concern whether or not the capsule was lost, even if that capsule did represent more than two million dollars and countless hours of work. To be completely just, the thousands of workers who had put together that capsule and the millions of citizens who had paid for it in tax dollars echoed Dee O'Hara's sentiments:

"What's money compared to a human life?"

The astronaut was picked up. The crisis was past.

"Give me something to blow my nose," he requested. "My head's full of sea water."

The capsule was gone. The helicopter managed to hook into the eye of the space vehicle, but the weight of water inside was too much. *Liberty Bell* 7

every light in the city had been turned on, every street sign, every neon sign, every house light. Bed sheets had been rigged to reflect the lights.

"Thank everybody," Glenn requested as he sped on his way.

Time passed. More time. Then the astronaut captured the hearts of everyone when he made his famous, lighthearted request for overtime pay.

But then, through no fault of his own, he scared the hearts out of everyone. The whole world knew he was in danger, but no one realized it as completely as the group in the blockhouse and those at the tracking stations.

For agonizing minutes, it seemed that the flight was doomed to end in tragedy, a nightmare become real. And there wasn't one thing the medical support team could do to help Glenn.

As *Friendship* 7 traveled between Hawaii and the West Coast of the United States, a signal was received. The heat shield of the capsule had apparently unlatched. This wasn't supposed to happen until the capsule was descending by parachute. The heat shield was the blunt forward end. It was made of Fiberglas-like material, designed to dispel the terrific friction heat that occurs on re-entry into the earth's atmosphere. It should, properly, char in the process.

But without the shield, the capsule itself would char. Without that shield, the pilot would be charred, too. Waiting to see if Glenn would live through it was the most ghastly experience of Dee O'Hara's life.

Friendship 7 landed at 1443 (2:43 P.M.), four hours and fifty-six minutes after launch, about 700 miles southeast of the Cape. John Glenn was alive. Miraculously, the alarm had turned out to be a false one.

Astronaut Glenn elected to remain inside his capsule until he was picked up. He was recovered by the destroyer *Noa* at 1504 (3:04 P.M.).

"It was hot in there," he remarked as he exited from his spaceship.

The country went wild over John Glenn Jr. He was the perfect hero. He was young, good-looking, and calm—and he had a sense of humor and modesty that endeared him to everyone who listened to his speeches, impromptu and planned.

He described his view of a phenomenon. He had seen various phosphorescent particles out in space. They had seemed rather like fireflies. He had reported them during debriefing.

But, he told the vast television audience, with a grin, the psychologist who examined him after his flight had been a bit skeptical. He'd asked, "What did they *say,* John?"

After the period of fear for Glenn's safety, there was naturally even more tension with the next launch. Grissom had had a close call. Glenn a closer one.

They were "the fellows," these astronauts. More than national heroes, they—John Glenn and the rest—were Dee's friends

Now it was Scott Carpenter's turn. The date was 24 May, 1962.

To another astronaut, this must have been a day of terrible disappointment and frustration. Deke Slayton had been scheduled for the flight, but the medical support team had detected a minor heart murmur.

Dee felt sick when she saw the results of that test. Deke had spent months and months of preparation, training, testing, of anticipation and then—nothing—washed out when the big moment was at hand. She tried her best to console Deke. Slayton himself was eager to go through with the mission, nevertheless. Permission was refused for his own protection.

So it was Carpenter who was launched at 0845 (8:45 A.M.), forty-five minutes behind schedule. He orbited the earth three times, traveling some 81,000 miles in about five hours, in his capsule, *Aurora 7.*

Then the medical support team and the waiting world suffered almost an hour's anguish. Radio communications were expected to black out part way down the descent, but only for four or five minutes. The blackout occurred on schedule—but it went on and on and on.

Almost immediately, it was known that *Aurora 7* had survived re-entry. But there was no indication at all as to the fate of the astronaut—safe or . . . The time was 1341 (1:41 P.M.)

Carpenter was picked up some hours later. He had been waiting, bobbing around in a life raft. The blackout had been caused by an overshoot of the target area. Coming down, the astronaut had been carried 250 miles beyond the intended Caribbean site, where the recovery ships waited.

It was another false alarm, but it created every bit as much tension as if it had been a real catastrophe. Dee O'Hara felt limp—again. Another one of "the fellows," Scott Carpenter, had achieved immortality and had lived to tell the tale.

"I feel fine," he remarked after he was picked up.

And for John Glenn's benefit—and for science—he noted the presence of "fireflies."

Another success, and it was time again for Dee O'Hara to go back to her duties, assisting with tests, keeping records—and keeping her apprehensions to herself. It was time again to watch the over-all morale.

It was up to Dee to keep worries and annoyances away from her charges—even to the point of refusing admittance to two workers who insisted that the air-conditioning unit in Hangar S needed repairing.

"It was fixed yesterday," she reminded them firmly. "The fellows" might be heroes, but they weren't goldfish in a bowl to be watched by the curious.

Then the date was 3 October, 1962. The man sitting on top of that rocket was Walter Schirra Jr.—full of fun, except where his mission was concerned, deadly serious about his mission in the *Sigma 7*, gregarious until near flight time, then requesting privacy.

He made six orbits and traveled 160,000 miles in nine hours and nearly fourteen minutes. As he flew over Hawaii, he called out "Aloha." When he got the go-ahead for six orbits, he shouted, "Hallelujah!"

This was the longest flight to date.

The trip was incredible. Problems were minimal. Schirra made a near-bull's-eye landing. He came down within 4 miles of the carrier *Kearsage,* 330 miles northeast of Midway Island, in the Pacific.

"That's a sweet little bird," he said of *Sigma 7*.

One to go. All of "the fellows" were safe but one. Had they run out of luck, Dee wondered? No, of course not. Each one had proved himself capable. Each capsule had functioned. But who could be certain, this time, with a longer trip planned? If only she could be *sure,* she could really enjoy it to the hilt.

The date was 15 May, 1963. Gordon Cooper was on deck. He was ready to go for twenty-two orbits.

Suppose, at the very end, there was a disaster?

It could have ended that way. The automatic controls failed. Astronaut Cooper took over the manual controls and landed. He not only made his re-entry, he made a bull's-eye, 15 miles east-southeast of Midway, close to the *Kearsage.*

Mission completed. America had gone for broke and had won. There were parades, celebrations, festivities. There were Distinguished Service Medals for the astronauts. There was knowledge that many thousands of workers had done their jobs well. And—there was something very special for Dee O'Hara.

As First Lady of Rose Festival, Dee was greeted by her proud mother

Chapter 9

SPOTLIGHT
ON
DEE

A message from Portland reached Dee soon after the first of the manned spacecraft flights, the historic event on 5 May, 1961, starring Alan Shepard.

Reading it, Dee could hardly believe her eyes. Here was another link in the fantastic chain of events. It was an invitation to the annual Rose Festival. It was more than that. It was an invitation to preside at the week-long event as First Lady of the Rose Festival.

Imagine! The girl who called Crabtree her home town and who called Portland her home city was invited back as a celebrity.

What fabulous fun! For a minute, Dee gave her imagination free rein, picturing the way it would be. Then she brought her wits back to earth.

"I can't accept," she said.

"Why not?" asked Shirley Sineath.

"Because they've got it all wrong," Dee answered. "It's Al Shepard who's the hero. I'm no heroine. I didn't do anything—only my job."

"That's exactly what Al Shepard was doing, too —his job," Shirley pointed out.

"But he's the one who took the risk," argued the girl with the pixie hairdo.

"He and a few thousand missile workers and the Pan Am nurses—and—" her roommate snorted. "And all the others. It would take a book to just list all the names. You said yourself, over and over, that it was a team effort. Aren't you part of the team?"

"And you said yourself that every American was on the team," someone else chimed in.

"But—but it would look as if I were trying to grab off a little personal glory," Dee said. "That's phony, letting people think—I can't *stand* phonies—"

"For once in your life, quit being so modest," her friends told her. "No matter how you slice it, you *are* the first aerospace nurse. You have been actively involved in Project Mercury. It's a fact. It's history, whether or not you want to claim credit."

And, they told her, it was perfectly natural for her home city to want to honor her. How else could Portland claim its share of the credit? If each American had a stake in Project Mercury, then each town had the right, the need, to publicly point with pride when one of its own had been there, through the long months of preparation and during the actual flight.

"You owe it to Portland," Shirley announced firmly. "You'd short-change Portland if you refuse. Besides, it's your duty to build up the feeling of active participation and personal involvement for every American, whenever you get the chance."

"All right, when you put it that way," Dee agreed. Having made her decision, she might as well enjoy it to the hilt. It would be another improbable adventure in the saga of Dee O'Hara. Her Irish eyes began to sparkle in anticipation.

She sent her acceptance and thanks to Ed Casey, president of the Rose Festival Association. Then, dressed in her Air Force uniform, she boarded the plane. Her heart lifted. For the first time since she'd been commissioned, she was going home. Now that she was on her way, she realized how much she had missed Oregon and all her friends back home.

During the months of work on Project Mercury, the months of traveling and making speeches and of presiding over Hangar S, she had been too busy to be homesick. Besides, during those months of intensive activity, her personal concerns had been set aside. Her total concentration had been given to "the fellows," to her job.

Now she could hardly wait. She was going home at long last.

She didn't know exactly what to expect when

she arrived. The reception was beyond her wildest expectations. There was a crowd to meet her at the airport and Mr. Casey presented her with an enormous bunch of roses. Flash-bulbs popped.

There were Jenny O'Hara and Bill, faces reflecting their pride. Tears started up in Dee's eyes. Unconsciously, she glanced around, looking for the other member of the family. The missing one. Big Mick O'Hara with the wavy black hair and the laughing blue eyes. If only—

"He knows," murmured her mother, a catch in her voice.

Dee was whisked off with her escort, Lorne Greene, the television star. Imagine the girl from Crabtree riding along in a convertible with the man known to millions as "Ben Cartwright" in the TV series "Bonanza." Imagine bands, imagine the Rose Festival parade going through the streets of Portland, with Dee O'Hara as the guest of honor, waving to the crowds lining the parade route!

She almost fell out of the car at one point. Right there, on the corner, were a couple of girls she'd known at Providence Hospital School of Nursing. Laughing and crying, they shouted greetings.

Who would have dreamed, just a short time ago, that the probie from Providence—the student nurse who had managed to get practically impaled on the iron spikes at the top of a gate on her way back to the Nurses' Residence after hours—would wind up like this?

That Rose Festival week was a week to remember, a fairy-tale week. There was a lacrosse game in the city's new colosseum. It didn't matter which team won the game because the crowds were really celebrating another sort of victory, the victory that all America shared, the success of the first phase of the conquest of space. There were dinners and all sorts of functions and festivities.

Afterward, Dee was glad she had let herself be persuaded to accept the invitation. She had the time of her life, and she could see with her own eyes that her mere presence did indeed bring Project Mercury closer to the citizens of Portland.

The next year she had no qualms about accepting another invitation to preside as First Lady of the Rose Festival. That second year there was even more reason for celebration. Grissom, Glenn, and Carpenter had made their historic flights into space.

Project Mercury was going forward. Sometimes it seemed as if it were rushing toward completion too fast. Once it was over, what about Dee O'Hara? Would NASA take her along to the new Manned Spacecraft Center now under construction at Houston, Texas, where the Gemini program would be centered? Would the Air Force call her back to duty? What?

Well, there was no point in worrying about it—

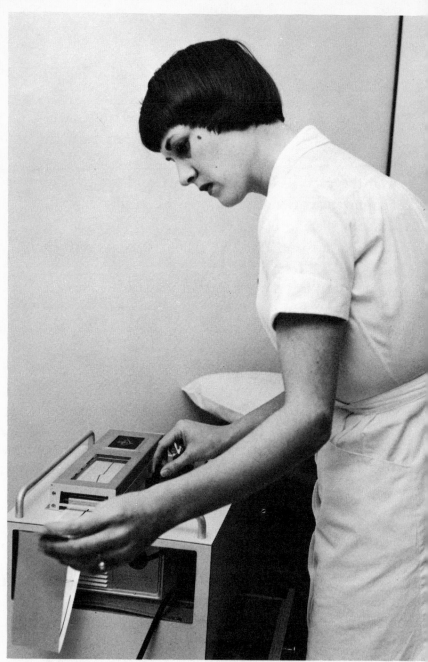

Working in her quarters at the Manned Spacecraft Center, Houston, Dee O'Hara operates electrocardiogram equipment

not yet—not even when the astronauts began moving their families to Houston in July of 1962. Time would tell. Now, she still had more than enough to keep her busy at the Cape. It was time to sort out all she'd learned about the duties of an aerospace nurse.

Fact sheets were compiled by flight surgeons, too. Future aerospace physicians would benefit from knowledge obtained during the flights of Project Mercury. Earthbound physicians should also have access to such information, for some of it would be applicable to the treatment of diseases here on earth.

Dee also had her regular duties to carry out as a member of the medical support team. Schirra and Cooper still had scheduled flights to make. Then it was all over. Project Mercury was completed.

The time had come to make the decision. If Dee were to continue to work with NASA, she must belong to NASA instead of being on loan from the Air Force. Give up her commission? Resign?

It was a difficult decision and it took a lot of soul-searching. But, for four years she had been committed to the manned space flight group. She resigned her commission, with quite a few pangs. She was a civilian again, separated from the Air Force as far as active duty was concerned, but never separated from her many friends in service. Then—stalemate.

The Manned Spacecraft Center wasn't completed yet. There was no place for Dee O'Hara. With facilities not ready for a huge influx of personnel, there was a temporary freeze on hiring.

Even if NASA had been able to hire her, Dee wouldn't have been willing to simply languish on a payroll, with nothing to do. She crossed her fingers, hoped for the best, and took a job as office nurse for a doctor at Cocoa Beach. At least she'd be busy, she'd be working with patients and she'd be close to her friends at the Cape and at Patrick AFB. And at least she knew NASA wanted her and wasn't trying to ease her out.

It was a long wait, from August 1963 when she resigned her commission until March 9, 1964, when she moved to Houston. It was old home week in Houston. She was back with "the fellows," their families, and the medical team—back where she belonged.

Her new base of operations was in the Manned Spacecraft Center, a huge complex of thirty buildings located on 1,620 acres of land, an astonishing place that almost defied imagination.

Building 8: Technical Services, Flight Medicine and Occupational Health Branches of Center Medical Operations, a part of the Center Medical program directed by Dr. Charles A. Berry, was Dee O'Hara's bailiwick. She loved the place on sight. Sunny, soft muted colors, wide expanses, enormous windows, and glass doors. This was one building she could find with-

New centrifuge chamber at the Manned Spacecraft Center is a backdrop for NASA nurse Dee O'Hara, as she reports for duty

out a map. Of course, she familiarized herself with the others, for all phases of work dovetailed—all were concerned with Project Gemini and Project Apollo.

Building 29 had importance for Dee for here are the circular centrifuge and chamber area. The astronauts would ride in a gondola measuring 12 feet in diameter, three at a time. At the end of the 50-foot arm, they could be whirled at 20 to 30 G's (gravity) for training. Their reactions would be recorded.

This was the world of Dee O'Hara. And here she would work with "the fellows," who now numbered more than the original seven. Nine more had been selected in September 1962.

They were a bit younger than the first astronauts, since Projects Gemini and Apollo would last longer than Mercury. Thirty-five was the top age. The second group also had to meet stiffer academic qualifications. Much of the guesswork had been removed by the original pilots; now astronauts would be required to conduct more difficult scientific procedures and studies in flight.

Reviewing their records, Dee had no need to wonder if they'd be "human." The first ones were and now they and their families were among her dearest friends. She knew, too, that they'd been chosen not only because they'd each had more than 1,500 hours of flying time, not only because they possessed degrees in engineering but because they were emotionally stable and all were very strongly motivated.

They included Neil Armstrong, Frank Borman, Charles Conrad Jr., James Lovell Jr., James A. McDivitt, Elliot M. See Jr., Thomas P. Stafford, Edward H. White, and John Young.

A third group of astronauts were chosen in October of 1963, so Dee O'Hara had thirty charges in all.

The group now included: Capt. Michael Collins, U.S.A.F.; R. Walter Cunningham, a research physicist; Capt. Donn F. Eisele, U.S.A.F.; Capt. Theodore C. Freeman, U.S.A.F.; Lt. Comdr. Richard F. Gordon, U.S.N.; Russell L. Schweickart, a research scientist from M.I.T.; Capt. David R. Scott, U.S.A.F.; Capt. Clifton C. Williams Jr., U.S.M.C.; Maj. Edwin E. Aldrin Jr., U.S.A.F.; Capt. William A. Anders, U.S.A.F.; Capt. Charles A. Bassett II, U.S.A.F.; Lt. Alan L. Bean, U.S.N.; Lt. Eugene A. Cernan, U.S.N.; Lt. Robert B. Chaffee, U.S.N.

Most of the astronauts moved their families into homes in the Seabrook area, out past the Center. Dee O'Hara took an apartment near the city proper, bringing much of her Florida home atmosphere to Houston.

The close-knit group shrank by one. John Glenn would remain as a consultant, but would no longer be an active participant. He was running for the United States Senate. Across the country, enthusiastic admirers predicted a landslide victory. But the first American to orbit the earth became a victim of a very common

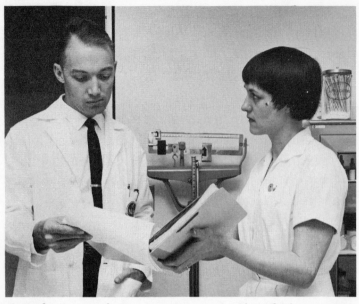

Consultation with Dr. Jernigan and other flight surgeons constitutes part of Dee's work in the Flight Medicine unit

accident. He slipped, in a hotel, struck his head and was ill for too long to continue the race for U.S. senator.

Then real tragedy struck the group.

The astronauts underwent constant, rigorous training, conditioning their bodies and minds to flights in space. It was vital, however, that they keep up their actual flying skills. When not otherwise occupied, they flew from nearby Ellington Air Force Base.

It was on such a routine training flight that the disaster occurred. News was relayed to Dee O'Hara that a plane had crashed. Her chief, Dr. Berry, and others dashed to the scene. Until they saw with their own eyes, they had no way of knowing the victim's identity.

It was Ted Freeman. One of "the fellows."

A snow goose had somehow collided with the plane as Astronaut Freeman came in for a landing.

Shattered Plexiglas was sucked up by the plane engines. Power failed. The plane crashed. But not until after Astronaut Freeman changed directions, deliberately veered so his plane, now a lethal weapon, would land away from buildings and from innocent bystanders. That second that it took to change direction was probably what cost him his life. When he ejected, there wasn't sufficient altitude for his parachute to operate effectively.

There was nothing that Dr. Berry could do. He had given his life for his country, for Project Gemini, just as surely as if he had flown in space.

Eye in the sky: photo of a galaxy some 8 million light years away

Chapter 10

LOOKING AHEAD

The news of Ted Freeman's death traveled like a shock wave. That wave touched everyone, down to the youngest clerk at the Manned Spacecraft Center. It touched every citizen outside the complex.

Those who knew him best—the medical group, the other astronauts, the nurse—did the two positive things indicated.

They gathered around the stunned wife of the missing member of the team—for she, too, was very definitely a part of that team. Dee's heart went out to the young woman who was her friend, not because part of her responsibility lay in guarding the morale of the team, but through genuine affection.

And they all went back to work. This was the way they could prove, for all time, the importance of Astronaut Freeman's contribution. The progress and ultimate success of the space program would be a perpetual memorial.

Step by giant step, as Project Gemini and Project Apollo move forward, as other projects are instituted, the names of all of them will be there, in history. They are the pioneers.

The story of the conquest of space has just begun and yet the dream began centuries ago. As far back as 160 B.C., a concept of the universe, with Earth in a minor role, was depicted in Cicero's "Republic." In A.D. 160, Lucian of Greece wrote a story of a flight to the moon. In more recent times, Voltaire, Dumas, Jules Verne, Edgar Allan Poe, and H. G. Wells contributed to the imagined flights in space.

A novel of a man-made satellite in orbit, "The Brick Moon," was published in 1869. Its author was Edward Everett Hale, famous for another novel, "The Man Without a Country."

Rockets, the forerunners of manned space vehicles, go far back into history. The first on record were used in A.D. 1232 in China to repel an attack by Mongols. Rockets were used in the Napoleonic Wars and in the War of 1812. A rocket device to carry a line to a disabled vessel and rescue the crew by breeches buoy was patented in 1838.

At the turn of this century, Konstantin Ziolkovsky, a Russian, projected the theory of space travel, utilizing liquid fuel rockets. Hermann Oberth spurred experimental rocket research in Germany with the publication of his book, "The Rocket into Interplanetary Space," in 1923.

An American, Dr. Robert H. Goddard, launched the world's first liquid fuel rocket on March 16, 1926, to a distance of 184 feet. In 1929 he launched the first instrumented rocket, with a barometer, a thermometer, and a small camera aboard. By 1935 he had launched rockets to 7,500 feet and speeds of more than 700 miles an hour.

The first man-made satellite, Sputnik I, was placed in orbit by Russia on October 4, 1957. Explorer I was launched by the U.S. on January 31, 1958.

Then came the manned spacecraft programs.

And Dee O'Hara became the first aerospace nurse. She was appointed to a unique place in history.

Just as the story of manned space flight is merely beginning with the successful completion of Project Mercury, so the story of Dee O'Hara is merely beginning. Who can tell where her adventures will lead her and "the fellows"?

For the present, Dee's work is cut out for her. She goes about her duties at the Manned Spacecraft Center, assisting with the countless, complicated tests and checks of the astronauts. She collects data and keeps records that will be used for increasing understanding of aerospace medicine, of man's reaction to the hostile environment of outer space.

Dr. Milton Matters, NASA medical test monitor, checks on Astronaut Schweickhart prior to simulated Gemini re-entry

When the time comes for the Gemini and Apollo teams to go to Cape Kennedy for launching, she will be there, on the job as a member of the medical team, helping to monitor the life-support systems.

Various dials and gauges will relay back the second-by-second condition of the men inside the capsules. On the basis of those reports, and the flight crews' verbal messages, the medical team will provide long-distance care. Perhaps an astronaut will be ordered to take medication to overcome some adverse reaction. Perhaps he will be ordered back to earth.

Inevitably, as the projects progress, Dee is sought out for interviews.

"What are the astronauts like?" the public wants to know.

"Great," she answers. "Wonderful."

"What makes them such super men? Are they born that way? Different from ordinary mortals?"

"They're highly intelligent, of course," she says thoughtfully. "They're emotionally stable and physically healthy. They have tremendous knowledge of the sciences and great skills in flying.

"Maybe what sets them apart is simple. Look at their records. They're people who never sat back and waited for tickets for free rides on the gravy train. Look at the tremendous effort each one made to get formal education, to become a top pilot, to stay in condition—not just when they wanted to apply here.

but way back. Every step of the way, each one put out tremendous effort to learn, to be good at each job as it came along. They *earned* their appointments."

"Maybe that's why you get along with them so well, why there's no friction," a shrewd observer remarks. "You're cut out of the same cloth."

What about the future—for aerospace nursing, for Dee O'Hara herself?

Sooner or later, there will be a nurse in space. Already, nurses are preparing for that day. Will that first nurse in space be Dee O'Hara? "At present I have no plans to travel in space," Dee says.

Notice that wording. "At present." Dee hasn't closed the door against such a possibility. She's not a door closer—never has been. Notice the sparkle in her eyes—the flair for adventure in her past.

That first nurse in space may or may not be Dee O'Hara. One thing is certain, however. Whoever she is, that first nurse will be there because Dee paved the way. Despite her modesty, she cannot deny the fact that she is part of history; the history of nursing, the history of the world, the history of space flight.

She ranks with Florence Nightingale, the Lady with the Lamp, who worked out the principles of modern nursing; with Dorothea Dix, who formulated the principles of nursing in prisons and in military hospitals during the Civil War; with Clara Barton,

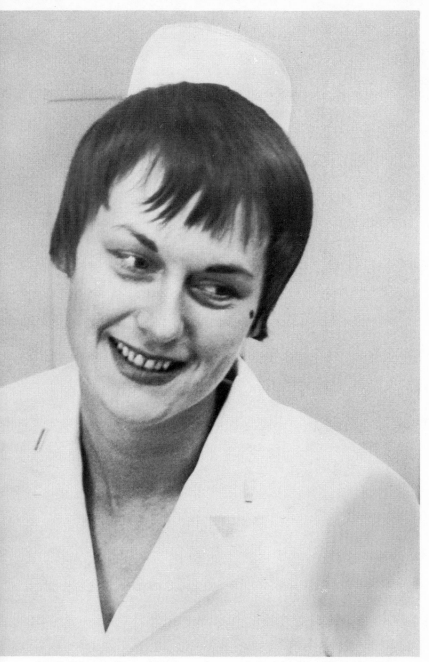

NASA nurse Dee O'Hara, who works with the astronauts of Projects Gemini and Apollo—America's first aerospace nurse

founder of the American Red Cross, who mapped out wartime and disaster nursing procedures; with Mary Breckinridge, founder of the Frontier Nursing Service in Kentucky, the "Nurses on Horseback," who established the first school for nurse-midwives in the United States.

Dee O'Hara laid the foundations for aerospace nursing. She earned the right by doing her best at each level of her life.

Like her illustrious predecessors, she was "just doing her job."